LANGUAGE!®

The Comprehensive Literacy Curriculum

ASSESSMENT: TEACHER EDITION

BOOK A

Administering, Scoring, and Interpreting:

- **Baseline Assessment**
- **Ongoing Assessment**
- **Summative Assessment**

Jane Fell Greene, Ed.D.

Sopris West®

A Cambium Learning® Company

BOSTON, MA • LONGMONT, CO

12 11 10 09 8 7 6 5 4 3 2

Authors:
Jane Fell Greene, Ed.D.
Nancy Chapel Eberhardt

ISBN 10 digit: 1-60218-666-9
ISBN 13 digit: 978-1-60218-666-8

Printed in the United States of America

Published and distributed by

Sopris West®
EDUCATIONAL SERVICES

A Cambium Learning® Company

4093 Specialty Place • Longmont, CO 80504 • (303) 651-2829
www.sopriswest.com

169105/9-08

Table of Contents

Assessments Overview

Ongoing Assessments

End-of-Book Content Mastery

Baseline Assessments and Progress Indicators

Appendices

Assessment Overview

- Placement
- Baseline Assessment
- Ongoing Assessment
- Summative Assessment

Welcome to the *LANGUAGE!* Assessment System

The *LANGUAGE!* Assessment System is a well-designed, efficient assessment system that provides teachers with the measures they need to accurately place students into the curriculum and to monitor, in a timely fashion, their progress through the curriculum. It furnishes the teacher with the data necessary to inform instruction and to ensure that each student meets his or her goals.

This system is comprised of formative and summative tests designed to capture skill development in the critical areas of literacy: phonemic awareness and phonics, spelling and word recognition, vocabulary and morphology, listening and reading comprehension, fluency, and speaking and writing. Consistent use of these assessments is critical to each student's success.

The following pages give a general overview of the system and tests contained therein. Information regarding the administration, scoring, and score interpretation for each test can be found in the specific test section of this book. The comparable information for Placement can be found in the *LANGUAGE! Reading Scale Placement Test: Teacher Edition* booklet.

The *LANGUAGE!* Assessment System

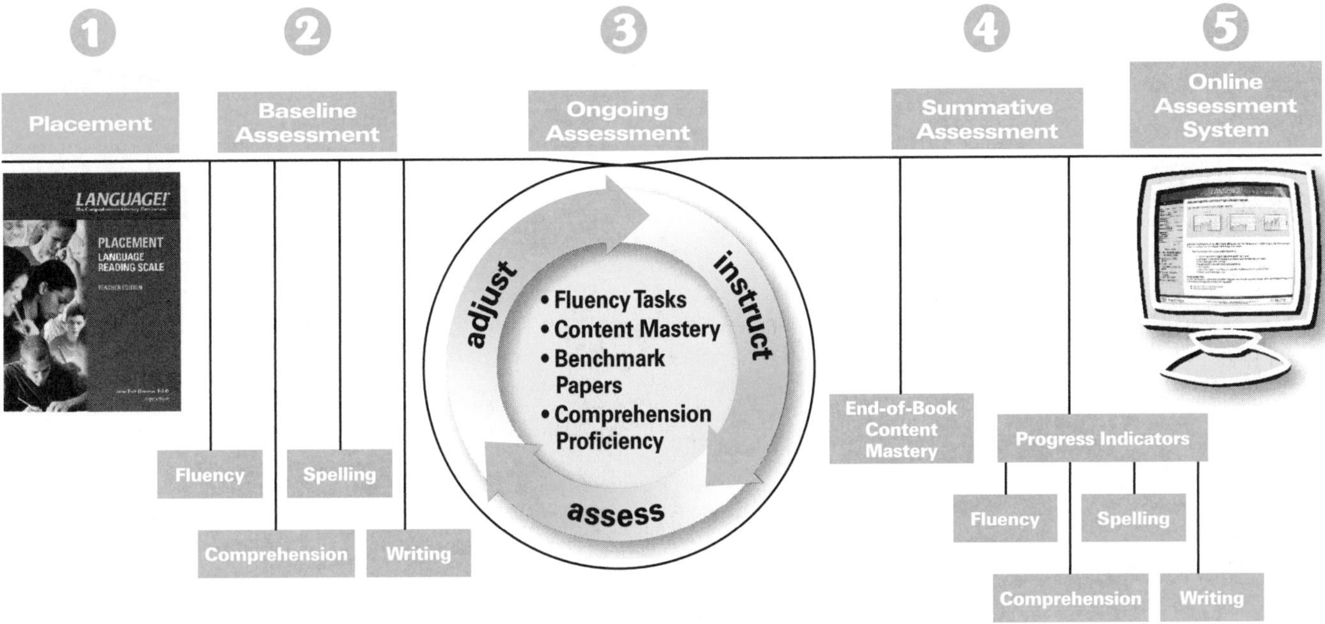

1 Placement

Data from the *LANGUAGE! Reading Scale Placement Test* indicates which of the three *LANGUAGE!* entry points is appropriate for each student.

2 Baseline Assessments

Administered only once after a student's placement in Book A, C, or E and prior to entering the *LANGUAGE!* curriculum, scores on baseline tests constitute the starting point for measuring a student's progress through the curriculum.

3 Ongoing Assessments

Regular testing of student mastery of the content, concepts, and skills taught in the curriculum ensures that teachers have current information about each student in order to adjust pacing or provide instructional support activities for individual students.

4 Summative Assessments

Given at the end of each book, the Summative Assessments assess the critical skills of literacy through both norm-referenced and curriculum-based measures.

5 The Online Assessment System

This easy-to-use database allows teachers and administrators to record, track, and report student test results. Teachers and administrators can monitor student growth through reports that can be generated at the individual, class, building, and district levels.

Placement

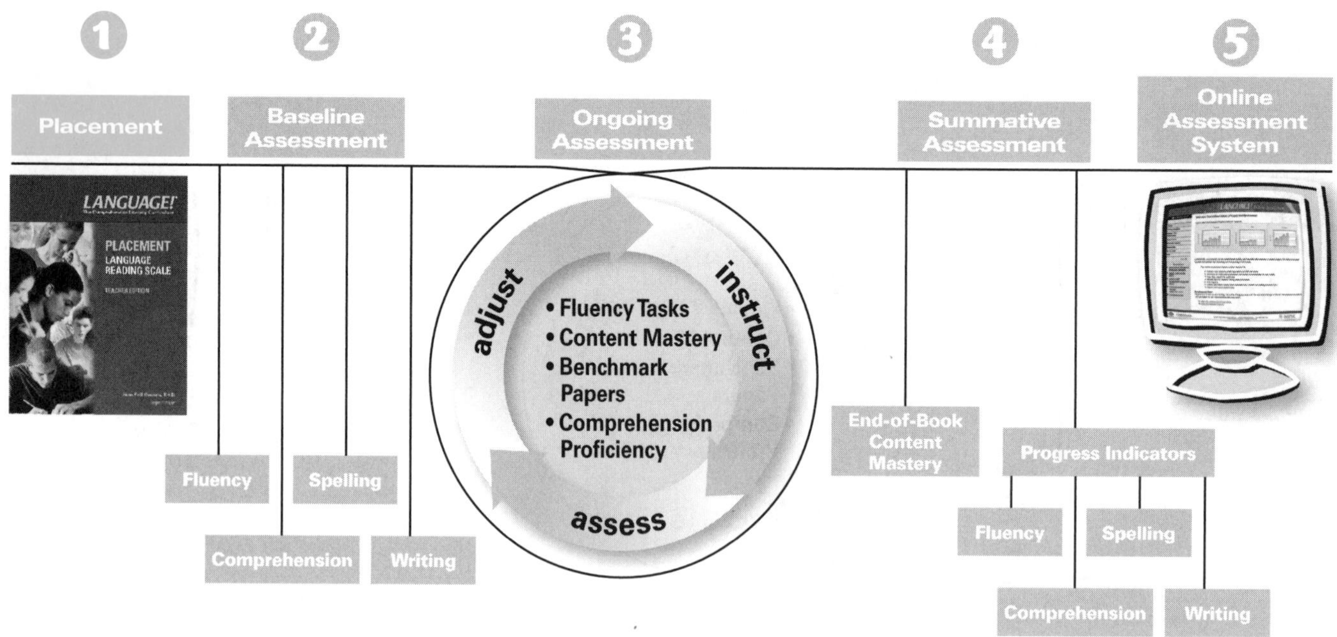

Accurate placement into *LANGUAGE!* is the first step to effective instruction. The *LANGUAGE! Reading Scale Placement Test* is a reading comprehension tool based on the Lexile readability scale. The results of this test determine which of the three *LANGUAGE!* entry points is appropriate for each student. The placement criteria can be found in the *LANGUAGE! Reading Scale Placement Test: Teacher Edition.*

LANGUAGE! Entry Points

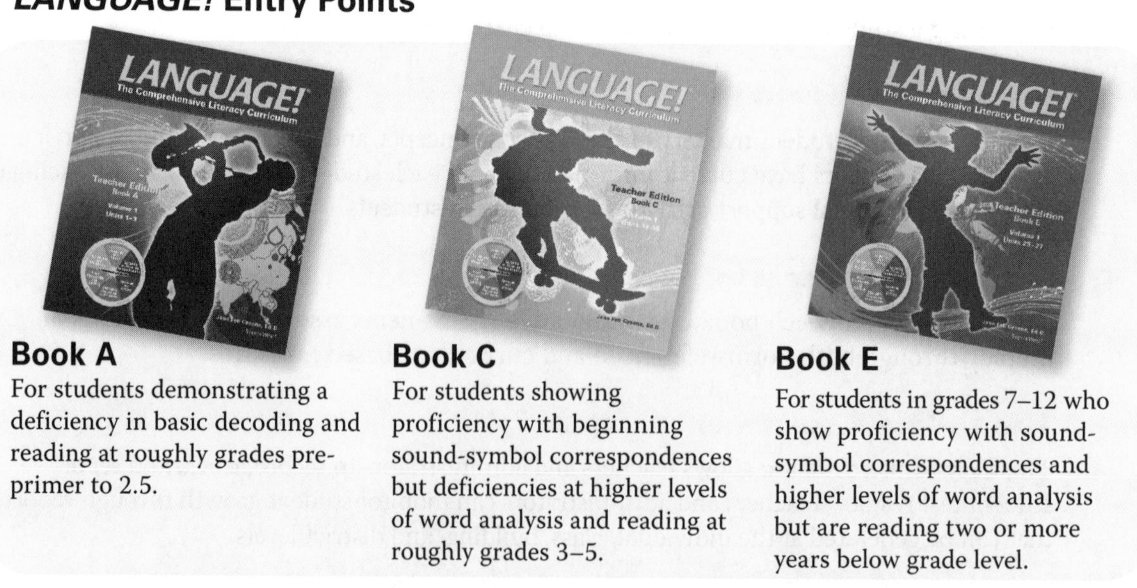

Book A
For students demonstrating a deficiency in basic decoding and reading at roughly grades pre-primer to 2.5.

Book C
For students showing proficiency with beginning sound-symbol correspondences but deficiencies at higher levels of word analysis and reading at roughly grades 3–5.

Book E
For students in grades 7–12 who show proficiency with sound-symbol correspondences and higher levels of word analysis but are reading two or more years below grade level.

Two Placement tests are available; *The LANGUAGE! Reading Scale Placement Test (Grades 3–5),* and *The LANGUAGE! Reading Scale Placement Test (Grades 6–12),* one of which should be selected according to the grade level of the students being tested. These tests utilize a multiple-choice format, are group administered and take approximately 45 minutes.

Baseline Assessment

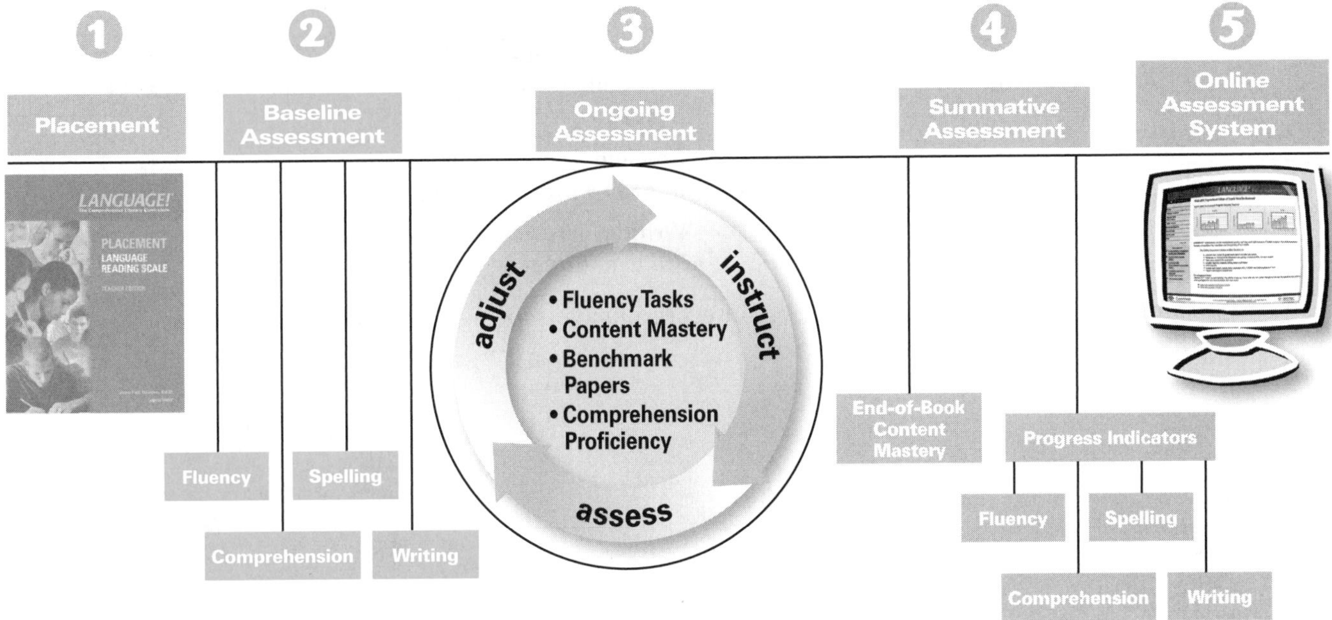

Purpose

The Baseline Assessments consist of four components that measure students' literacy skills. The Baseline Assessment is taken only once, immediately after students' entry into Book A, C, or E. These same tests are used as Progress Indicators as part of the Summative Assessments at the end of the book. The comparison of Baseline and Progress Indicator results allows teachers and students to measure students' growth in key literacy skills by the end of each book level.

These tests:

- Are only given once, immediately after a student's entry into Book A, C, or E
- Provide reliable and valid measures of contextual reading fluency, reading comprehension, spelling, and writing
- Guide the teacher's decision-making process about where to place instructional emphasis when beginning instruction in the curriculum
- Provide a baseline from which to measure growth

Assessment Overview

Baseline Assessments		Measures
Test of Silent Contextual Reading Fluency (TOSCRF)	Norm-referenced	**Fluency.** Contextual reading measuring speed and accuracy
LANGUAGE! Reading Scale	Lexile® based	**Comprehension.** Text comprehension, specifically the ability to construct meaning while reading a passage
TWS-4	Norm-referenced	**Spelling.** Dictated spelling, measuring the ability to spell words in written form
Writing	Rubric Based	**Writing.** Written expression based on the Six Traits of Effective Writing.

More information for administering, interpreting and scoring the Baseline tests can be found on page 57.

Ongoing Assessment

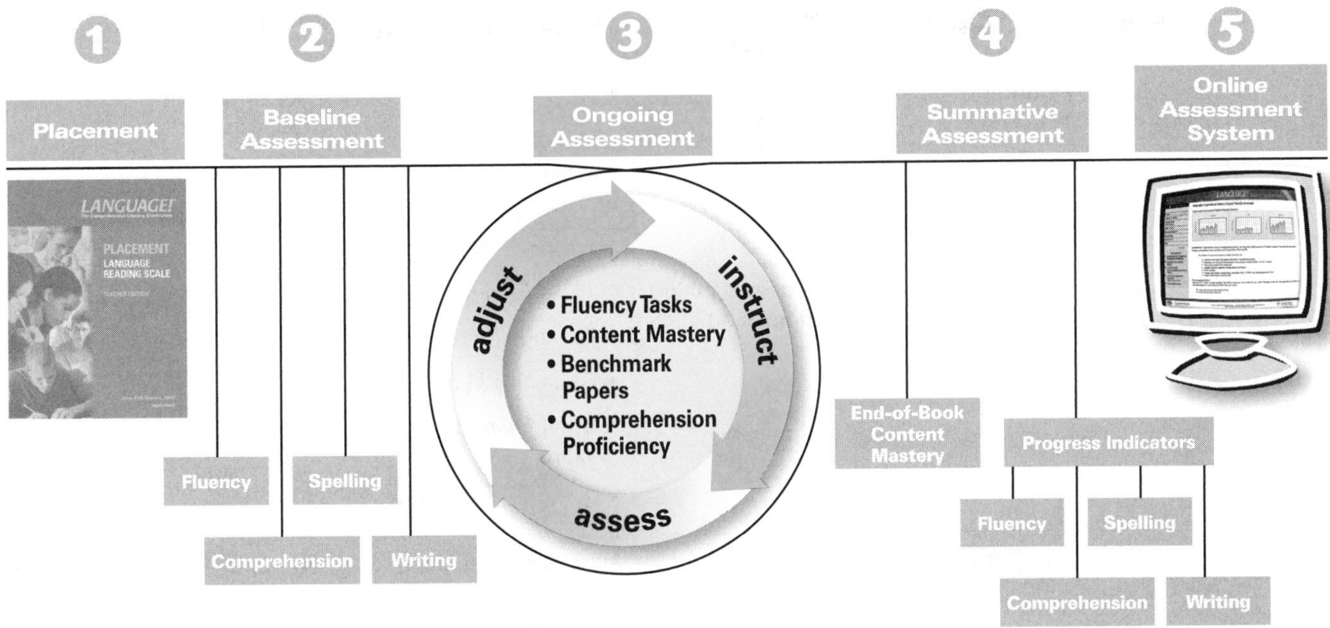

Purpose

In every unit of the *LANGUAGE!* curriculum, students complete designated Fluency, Content Mastery, Benchmark Papers for Writing, and Comprehension Proficiency tasks. Using these tools, teachers can assess students' acquisition of curriculum-based content.

These tests:

- Focus on specific content taught in each unit
- Emphasize recently taught content and concepts
- Give students practice in a variety of test formats, including multiple-choice, open-ended questions, written spelling, and paragraph and essay writing

Assessment Overview

Ongoing Assessment

Step	Test	Critical Skills Measured	Focus of Test Items	Format
1	Content Mastery	Phonemic Awareness and Phonics	• Sound-spelling correspondences • Syllable types • Morphology awareness	Recall/written response
2	• Fluency • Content Mastery	Word Recognition and Spelling	• Word Fluency • Passage Fluency • Spell Unit Words • Spell Essential Words • Spell affixed words	• Timed fluency • Spelling Test 1 (single words) • Spelling Test 2 (dictated sentences)
3	Content Mastery	Vocabulary and Morphology	• Word relationships (antonyms, synonyms, homophones, attributes) • Meaning of word parts	Multiple-choice
4	Content Mastery	Grammar and Usage	• Grammar • Sentence Structure	Multiple-choice
5	Comprehension Proficiency	Listening and Reading Comprehension	Reading comprehension (question interpretation, using text to answer questions)	• Multiple-choice • Short answer response
6	Benchmark Papers for Writing	Speaking and Writing	Written expression using the Six Traits of Effective Writing	Prompt-driven paragraph or essay writing

More information for administering, interpreting and scoring the Ongoing Assessment tests can be found on page 27.

Summative Assessment

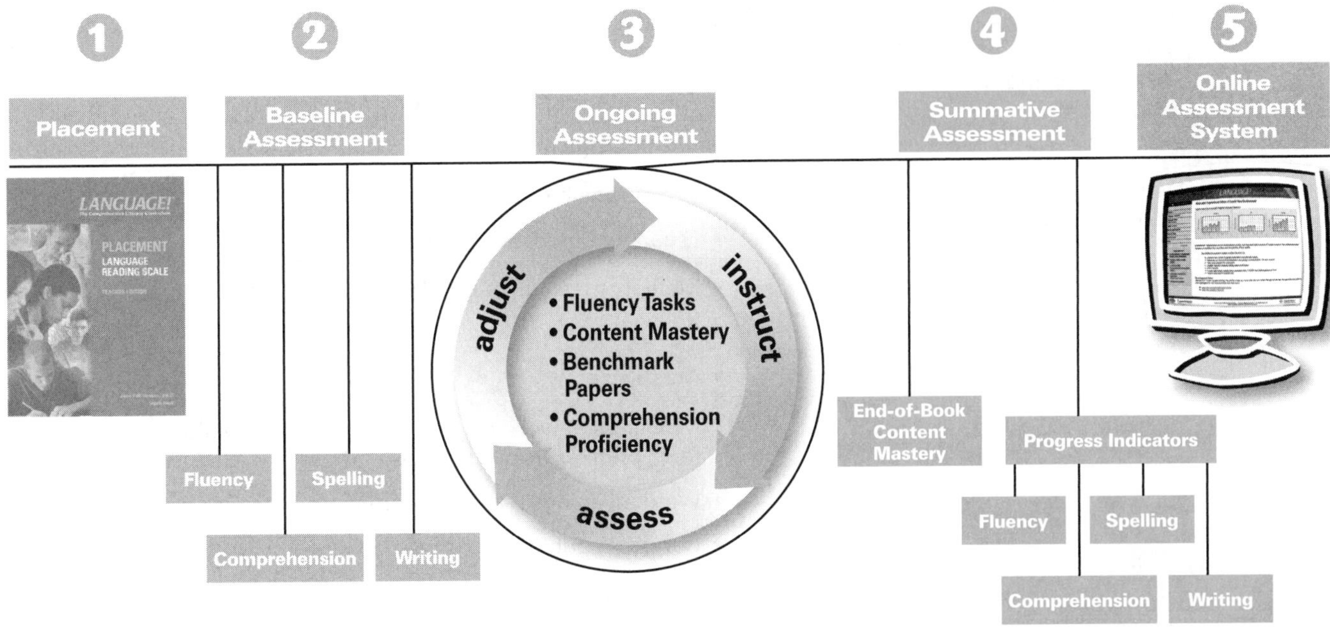

Purpose

At the end of each book, students complete the Summative Assessments to evaluate their overall acquisition of the curriculum content and to determine growth in key literary skills.

These tests:

The End-of-Book Content Mastery tests assess students' facility at integrating and applying curriculum-based content, concepts, and skills. They also give students additional practice with the kinds of test questions that appear on group-administered, standardized tests used by districts and states to monitor progress in reading, language, and writing.

End-of-Book Content Mastery

Critical Skills Measured		Focus of Test Items	Format
Phonemic Awareness and Phonics	Word Study	• Rhyme • Alternate spellings for phonemes • Morphological markers	• Multiple-choice
Vocabulary and Morphology	Vocabulary	• Definitions based on categorization • Meaning based on context	• Multiple-choice
	Word Relationships	• Multiple meaning of words • Synonyms • Antonyms	• Multiple-choice
	Morphology	• Meanings of word parts (e.g., prefixes, roots, suffixes) • Word meanings based on word parts • Correct usage of words with affixes	• Multiple-choice • Short answer
Grammar and Usage	Grammar	• Grammar	• Multiple-choice
	Sentence Structure	• Sentence Structure	

Progress Indicators

The Progress Indicators are an alternate form of the same tests as those given for the Baseline Assessments. These tests are designed to provide valid and reliable measures of speed and accuracy of word reading, reading comprehension, written spelling, and written expression. Because these are non-curriculum based measures, students cannot study the material in advance.

Progress Indicators		Measures
Test of Silent Contextual Reading Fluency (TOSCRF)	Norm-Referenced	**Fluency.** Recognition of individual words in a series of printed passages measuring speed and accuracy
LANGUAGE! Reading Scale	Criterion-Referenced Lexile®	**Comprehension.** Text comprehension, specifically the ability to construct meaning while reading a passage
TWS-4	Norm-Referenced	**Spelling.** Dictated spelling, measuring the ability to spell words in written form
Writing	Rubric based	**Writing.** Written expression based on the Six Traits of Effective Writing.

More information for administering, interpreting and scoring the Progress Indicator tests can be found on page 57.

The Online Assessment System

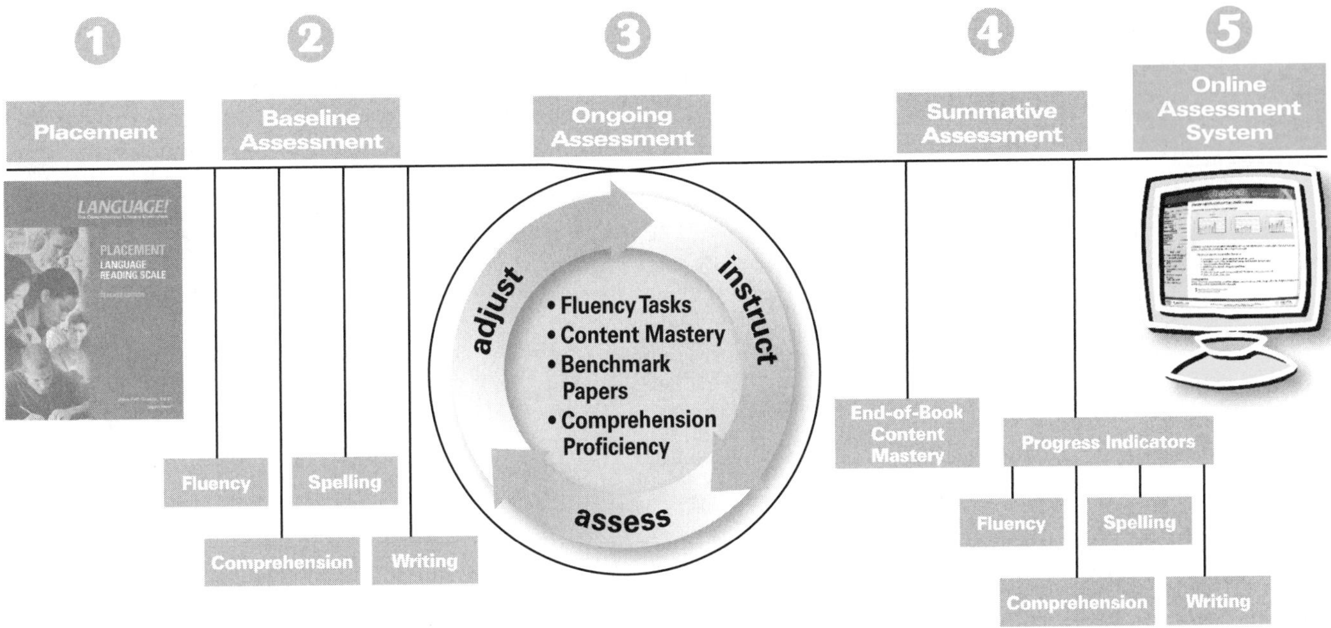

Purpose

The *Online Assessment System* is a powerful tool that supports placement, progress monitoring, and instructional pacing.

With the *Online Assessment System*, you can:

1. Obtain recommendations for student placement and pacing based on the raw scores entered
2. Automatically convert raw scores to grade equivalents and percentile ranks and save them for easy access
3. Track and monitor each student's performance from unit to unit
4. Create easy-to-read charts showing a student's growth in different target areas
5. Customize instruction to meet individual objectives and learning needs based on a review of student data
6. Generate and print reports for parents, students, teachers and administrators

LANGUAGE! Assessment Schedule Books A to F

The following chart outlines the assessment schedule for Content Mastery, Comprehension Proficiency, Benchmark Papers for Writing, End-of-Book Content Mastery and Progress Indicators for Books A through F. Baseline assessments are given only once, prior to student entry level.

	Unit	Key: Ongoing assessment (formative): Content Mastery (CM) Summative Assessment: End-of-Book Content Mastery (EOB CM) and Progress Indicators (PI)					
		Step 1: Phonemic Awareness and Phonics	Step 2: Word Recognition and Spelling	Step 3: Vocabulary and Morphology	Step 4: Grammar and Usage	Step 5: Listening and Reading	Step 6: Speaking and Writing
Book A	1	CM	CM: spelling	CM	CM		
	2	CM	CM: spelling	CM	CM		Benchmark paper
	3	CM	CM: spelling	CM	CM	Comprehension proficiency	
	4	CM	CM: spelling	CM	CM		Benchmark paper
	5	CM	CM: spelling	CM	CM	Comprehension proficiency	
	6	EOB CM: Multiple Choice	PI: TWS-4 PI: TOSCRF	EOB CM: Multiple Choice	EOB CM: Multiple Choice	PI: *LANGUAGE!* Reading Scale	PI: Writing
Book B	7	CM	CM: spelling	CM	CM		
	8	CM	CM: spelling	CM	CM		Benchmark paper
	9	CM	CM: spelling	CM	CM	Comprehension proficiency	
	10	CM	CM: spelling	CM	CM		Benchmark paper
	11	CM	CM: spelling	CM	CM	Comprehension proficiency	
	12	EOB CM: Multiple Choice	PI: TWS-4 PI: TOSCRF	EOB CM: Multiple Choice	EOB CM: Multiple Choice	PI: *LANGUAGE!* Reading Scale	Writing

	Unit	Key: Ongoing assessment (formative): Content Mastery (CM) Summative Assessment: End-of-Book Content Mastery (EOB CM) and Progress Indicators (PI)					
		Step 1: Phonemic Awareness and Phonics	Step 2: Word Recognition and Spelling	Step 3: Vocabulary and Morphology	Step 4: Grammar and Usage	Step 5: Listening and Reading	Step 6: Speaking and Writing
Book C	13	CM	CM: spelling	CM	CM		
Book C	14	CM	CM: spelling	CM	CM		Benchmark paper
Book C	15	CM	CM: spelling	CM	CM	Comprehension proficiency	
Book C	16	CM	CM: spelling	CM	CM		Benchmark paper
Book C	17	CM	CM: spelling	CM	CM	Comprehension proficiency	
Book C	18	EOB CM: Multiple Choice	PI: TWS-4 PI: TOSCRF	EOB CM: Multiple Choice	EOB CM: Multiple Choice	PI: *LANGUAGE!* Reading Scale	PI: Writing
Book D	19	CM	CM: spelling	CM	CM		
Book D	20	CM	CM: spelling	CM	CM		Benchmark paper
Book D	21	CM	CM: spelling	CM	CM	Comprehension proficiency	
Book D	22	CM	CM: spelling	CM	CM		Benchmark paper
Book D	23	CM	CM: spelling	CM	CM	Comprehension proficiency	
Book D	24	EOB CM: Multiple Choice	PI: TWS-4 PI: TOSCRF	EOB CM: Multiple Choice	EOB CM: Multiple Choice	PI: *LANGUAGE!* Reading Scale	PI: Writing

Assessment Overview

	Key: Ongoing assessment (formative): Content Mastery (CM) Summative Assessment: End-of-Book Content Mastery (EOB CM) and Progress Indicators (PI)						
	Unit	Step 1: Phonemic Awareness and Phonics	Step 2: Word Recognition and Spelling	Step 3: Vocabulary and Morphology	Step 4: Grammar and Usage	Step 5: Listening and Reading	Step 6: Speaking and Writing
Book E	25	CM	CM: spelling	CM	CM		
	26	CM	CM: spelling	CM	CM		Benchmark paper
	27	CM	CM: spelling	CM	CM	Comprehension proficiency	
	28	CM	CM: spelling	CM	CM		Benchmark paper
	29	CM	CM: spelling	CM	CM	Comprehension proficiency	
	30	EOB CM: Multiple Choice	PI: TWS-4 PI: TOSCRF	EOB CM: Multiple Choice	EOB CM: Multiple Choice	PI: *LANGUAGE!* Reading Scale	PI: Writing
Book F	31	CM	CM: spelling	CM	CM		
	32	CM	CM: spelling	CM	CM		Benchmark paper
	33	CM	CM: spelling	CM	CM	Comprehension proficiency	
	34	CM	CM: spelling	CM	CM		Benchmark paper
	35	CM	CM: spelling	CM	CM	Comprehension proficiency	
	36	EOB CM: Multiple Choice	PI: TWS-4 PI: TOSCRF	EOB CM: Multiple Choice	EOB CM: Multiple Choice	PI: *LANGUAGE!* Reading Scale	PI: Writing

Note: Content Mastery tasks are a variety of formats including multiple-choice, open-ended, and free recall.

Diagnostic Screening Instruments

Sometimes students fail to show much progress in critical skill areas, despite intensive intervention. In such cases, you may find additional diagnostic information necessary. Diagnostic screening tools, available outside the *LANGUAGE!* curriculum, can help to clarify the area of difficulty. The following chart identifies recommended diagnostic screening tools according to skill area.

Diagnostic Screening Instruments

Step in *LANGUAGE!*	Test Name	Description	Format	Norm-referenced?
Step 1 Phonemic Awareness and Phonics	**CTOPP: Comprehensive Test of Phonological Processing**[1]	*The Comprehensive Test of Phonological Processing* (CTOPP) assesses phonological awareness, phonological memory, and rapid naming. The CTOPP was developed to aid in the identification of individuals from kindergarten through college who may profit from instructional activities to enhance their phonological skills. The CTOPP can be used to: (a) to identify individuals who are significantly below their peers in important phonological abilities, and (b) to determine strengths and weaknesses among developed phonological processes.	Individual Administration Time to administer: 30 minutes	Yes
Step 2 Word Recognition and Spelling	**[Word Recognition]** **TOWRE: Test of Word Reading Efficiency**[2]	*The Test of Word Reading Efficiency* (TOWRE) is a nationally normed measure of word reading accuracy and fluency. Because it can be administered very quickly, the test provides an efficient means of monitoring the growth of two kinds of word reading skills that are critical in the development of overall reading ability: the ability to accurately recognize familiar words as whole units or "sight words" and the ability to "sound out" words quickly.	Individual Administration Time to administer: 5–10 minutes	Yes
	[Spelling] **WIAT-II: Wechsler Individual Achievement Test, Second Edition**[3]	*The WIAT-II Complete Test Battery* is a comprehensive yet flexible measurement tool useful for achievement skills assessment, learning disability diagnosis, special education placement, curriculum planning, and clinical appraisal for preschool children through adults. New norms also allow for the evaluation of and academic planning for college students with disabilities. *The WIAT-II Spelling Subtest* tasks vary with grade level. Students must correctly write dictated letters, letter blends, and words.	Individual Administration The Complete Test Battery: 1.5–2 hours	Yes

[1] Test information was gathered from ProEd, the test publisher's website: http://proedinc.com/customer/productView.aspx?ID=1615

[2] Test information was gathered from ProEd, the test publisher's website: http://proedinc.com/customer/productView.aspx?ID=1608

[3] Test information was gathered from Harcourt Assessment, Inc., the test publisher's website: http://harcourtassessment.com/HAIWEB/Cultures/en-us/Productdetail.htm?Pid=015-8983-505&Mode=summary

Diagnostic Screening Instruments				
Step in *LANGUAGE!*	Test Name	Description	Format	Norm-referenced?
Step 3 Vocabulary and Morphology	**[Vocabulary]** **EOWPVT: Expressive One-Word Picture Vocabulary Test**[4]	*The Expressive One-Word Picture Vocabulary Test* (EOWPVT) is an individually administered, norm-referenced test that provides an assessment of an individual's English speaking vocabulary. It is standardized for use with individuals ages 2-0 through 18-11.	Individual Administration Time to administer: 20 minutes	Yes
	[Vocabulary] **PPVT-4: Peabody Picture Vocabulary Test, Fourth Edition**[5]	*The Peabody Picture Vocabulary Test, Fourth Edition* (PPVT-4) scale is a norm-referenced, wide-range instrument for measuring the receptive (hearing) vocabulary of children and adults. Enlarged and colorized, this PPVT edition is available in two parallel forms (Form A and Form B) that are administered individually. Each form contains training items and 228 test items, each consisting of four full-color pictures as response options on a page. For each item, the examiner says a word, and the examinee responds by selecting the picture that best illustrates that word's meaning. The PPVT-4 scale measures understanding of the spoken word in standard American English and thus assesses vocabulary acquisition.	Individual Administration Time to administer: 10–15 minutes, although testing time varies case by case.	Yes
	[Morphology] **CELF-4: Clinical Evaluation of Language Fundamentals, Fourth Edition**[6]	*The Clinical Evaluation of Language Fundamentals-Fourth Edition* (CELF-4) gives you everything that you are looking for when evaluating a student's language performance. Combine core subtests with supplementary subtests to get a comprehensive assessment of a student's language skills. CELF is based on a four-level process model: Level 1 contains the four most discriminating subtests, enabling you to quickly determine whether or not there is a language disorder in one-third less time. At Level 2, you can administer norm-referenced subtests to examine a student's strengths and weaknesses across modalities and content areas. These subtests yield the following indexes: Receptive Language, Expressive Language, Language Content, Language Structure, and Language Memory.	Individual Administration Time to administer: 30–60 minutes	Yes, Level 2 subtests

[4] Test information was gathered from Harcourt Assessment, Inc., the test publisher's website: http://harcourtassessment.com/HAIWEB/Cultures/en-us/Productdetail.htm?Pid=015-8006-81X&Mode=summary

[5] Test information was gathered from Pearson Assessments, the test publisher's website: http://ags.pearsonassessments.com/group.asp?nGroupInfoID=a30700

[6] Test information was gathered from Harcourt Assessment, Inc., the test publisher's website: http://harcourtassessment.com/HAIWEB/Cultures/en-us/Productdetail.htm?Pid=015-8037-200&Mode=summary

Diagnostic Screening Instruments

Step in *LANGUAGE!*	Test Name	Description	Format	Norm-referenced?
Step 4 Grammar and Usage	**TROG-2: Test for Reception of Grammar, Version 2**[7]	*The Test for Reception of Grammar, Version 2* (TROG-2) is a fully revised and re-standardized version of the widely used TROG. TROG-2 evaluates the understanding of grammatical constructs, using a multiple choice format.	Individual Administration Time to administer: 10–20 minutes	Yes, based on UK 2001 Census
Step 5 Listening and Reading Comprehension	**[Reading Comprehension]** **GORT-4: Gray Oral Reading Tests, Fourth Edition**[8]	*The Gray Oral Reading Tests—Fourth Edition* (GORT-4) provides an efficient and objective measure of growth in oral reading and an aid in the diagnosis of oral reading difficulties.	Individual Administration Time to administer: 20–30 minutes	Yes
	[Reading Comprehension] **WRMT-R: Woodcock Reading Mastery Tests-Revised-(Normative Update)**[9]	*The Woodcock Reading Mastery Tests-Revised-Normative Update* (WRMT-R/NU) provide an expanded interpretive system and age range to help you assess reading skills of children and adults. Two forms, G and H, make it easy to test and retest, or you can combine the results of both forms for a more comprehensive assessment. Form G contains two readiness tests and four tests of reading achievement: Visual-Auditory, Learning, Letter Identification (and a Supplementary Letter Checklist), Word Identification, Word Attack, Word Comprehension (Antonyms, Synonyms, Analogies), Passage Comprehension. Form H contains four tests of reading achievement with parallel test items to Form G: Word Identification, Word Attack, Word Comprehension (Antonyms, Synonyms, Analogies), Passage Comprehension.	Individual Administration Time to administer: 10–30 minutes for each cluster of tests	Yes
	[Listening and Reading Comprehension] **WIAT-II**	See Step 2 Spelling Above	See Step 2 Spelling Above	See Step 2 Spelling Above

[7] Test information was gathered from Harcourt Assessment, Inc., the test publisher's website: http://harcourtassessment.com/HAIWEB/Cultures/en-us/Productdetail.htm?Pid=015-8075-34X&Mode=summary

[8] Test information was gathered from ProEd, the test publisher's website: http://proedinc.com/customer/productView.aspx?ID=690

[9] Test information was gathered from Pearson Assessments, the test publisher's website: http://ags.pearsonassessments.com/group.asp?nGroupInfoID=a16640

Recommended Testing Procedures

In any standardized or curriculum-based testing situation, there are regulatory and/or environmental elements to consider. Among them are the following:

1. Comply with local school policies and state regulations regarding test administration, interpretation, and issues of confidentiality.
2. If a student has a 504 plan or an Individualized Education Plan that calls for accommodations in a testing situation, make sure to implement the appropriate accommodations.
3. Provide an environment conducive to test taking including a quiet room, good lighting, appropriate furniture and writing tools.
4. Promote test-taking readiness by encouraging students to be well-rested and motivated.
5. Encourage students to do their best.
6. Review the specific directions for administration and scoring provided for each test.
7. Deliver the instructions for each test verbatim.
8. Students should not practice the tests or study the words or passages in the tests either before or after the tests are administered.
9. The assessments should not be used for teaching purposes; do not correct student's errors.
10. Keep the assessments in a secure place. Distribute the booklets immediately before testing, and collect them as soon as a testing session is done.

Sharing Performance Results with Students

Once students' Baseline, Ongoing, or Summative tests have been scored, confer with each student about his or her results. It is important for students to understand what their current skill levels are so they can see that growth has occurred or so they can establish goals for future learning.

Sharing Baseline Information with Students

Confer with individual students about their performance on Baseline measures. Walk the student through the results, pointing out his or her strengths and areas for improvement. During the feedback conversation, tell the student that Baseline tests document the current level of his or her skill development. Let the student know that upcoming instruction will help him or her remedy those areas of weakness that these tests have identified. The student will have multiple opportunities throughout the course of instruction to improve; the goal is for the student to show growth when the Progress Indicator results are compared to the Baseline scores.

Sharing Ongoing Assessment Information with Students

After students have completed the Ongoing Assessments, have a feedback conference with each student. Tell them that Ongoing Assessment results demonstrate acquisition of the content taught in specific units in the book. Outline the student's strengths first, and then walk him or her through areas that need improvement. Ask the student to think of steps to take to improve performance in areas where a weakness is indicated.

Sharing Summative Assessment Information with Students

After the Progress Indicator assessments have been scored, arrange to have individual conferences with students. During Progress Indicator feedback conversations, tell students that these tests show changes in their skill development when compared to their Baseline test scores (where available) or the Progress Indicator scores from the previous book. Start the conversation by focusing on areas where the student shows improvement, even if the gains are slight. Then point out the areas that still need improvement. Remind students that they will have an opportunity to improve in these areas as they continue in the curriculum and that they need to pay special attention to these areas of concern. Close the conversation with a reiteration of their gains. This is a time to encourage students to take pride in their accomplishments.

Using Student Performance Results to Inform Instructional Planning

Ideally, students' test results help inform classroom instruction. The more you understand with some precision the strengths and weaknesses of your class and of individual students, the more accurately and efficiently you can target instruction to students' needs.

- ***Using student scores to inform classroom instruction:***
  Examine the aggregated data on each test for your class, and look for patterns. If, for instance, most of the students scored low on the Test of Silent Contextual Reading Fluency (TOSCRF), you will want to weight classroom instruction and classroom time more toward Steps 1 and 2, Phonemic Awareness and Phonics and Word Recognition and Spelling, as you move into the next book.
- ***Using student scores to inform individual instruction:***
  If an examination of the class's aggregated scores reveals a few students who are deficient in a particular skill, as indicated by the assessment tests, there are many built-in opportunities in *LANGUAGE!* to address those weaknesses on a small-group or individual basis. You can turn to Homework Options, the Special Instructional Support material, or the If/Then boxes that follow each Content Mastery task in the book level Teacher Edition to provide additional practice in critical skills areas.

Meaningfully Home-School Communication

- Teachers can use assessment results as a basis for meaningful home-school communication. Providing this type of specific performance information helps parents or guardians understand what their child is learning and the skills he or she is developing.
- The *Teacher Resource Guide* provides letters to facilitate communication between school and home. Periodically arrange times to meet with parents or guardians to explain the connection between assessment results and the instruction provided in the curriculum. The more parents or guardians know about what their children are learning and understand the skills they are developing, the better prepared they are to support their students' learning efforts.

Exiting the Curriculum

When considering whether a student should exit from the *LANGUAGE!* curriculum, take into account the student's scores on both the End-of-Book Content Mastery test and the *LANGUAGE!* Reading Scale (LRS) Progress Indicator test. (Additionally, the data from the remaining Progress Indicators and Ongoing Assessment data should corroborate that a student has acquired the literacy content and skills needed to meet the requirements of content area courses.) The following are the criteria for exiting the program:

- Score of 80% or better on the End-of-Book Content Mastery test for the student's current book level
- Score within the Lexile® range designated for the student's grade level on the LRS test (see the chart below)

LANGUAGE! Exit Guidelines	
Grade level of student	Lexile® Reader Scale*
3	535–645
4	645–755
5	755–865
6	825–935
7	900–1020
8	945–1055
9	990–1100
10	1025–1135
11	1035–1145
12	1145–1155

*This range corresponds to the 50th percentile for the spring of the student's grade level, with +/- 55L to account for measurement error.

These levels of performance are required to assure that students are prepared to successfully meet grade level demands of content area courses and grade level state testing.

Ongoing Assessment

- Content Mastery
- Comprehension Proficiency
- Benchmark Papers for Writing
- Fluency

The Ongoing Assessment component of the *LANGUAGE!* Assessment System includes Content Mastery, Comprehension Proficiency, Benchmark Papers for Writing, and Fluency tasks. In each unit of the curriculum, students complete designated tasks that are designed to assess their acquisition of curriculum-based content.

Content Mastery

Description

Content Mastery tests for Steps 1 to 4 in *LANGUAGE!* focus on specific content taught in each unit in the critical skill areas of phonemic awareness and phonics, word recognition and spelling, vocabulary and morphology, and grammar and usage. With these tools, teachers can assess students' mastery of curriculum-based content.

Teachers administer these tests during the course of every unit in each of the different skill areas. The tests feature a variety of formats that give students practice with constructed responses and multiple choice questions.

Administering the Content Mastery Tasks

The unit lessons in the *Teacher Editions* for Books A–F provide teachers with the Content Mastery tasks and directions for administering them. Students complete Content Mastery tests in their *Assessment: Content Mastery* booklets. Teachers distribute the booklets to students immediately prior to the test and collect them when students finish the test.

Scores and Their Interpretation

- Teachers score the Content Mastery tasks, using the answers provided in the *Teacher Editions* at the point where the tests are administered.
- Mastery is set at 80 percent on each test. When there are multiple sections in a test, the 80 percent figure is based on the total score.
- When performance falls below 80 percent on a test, teachers should take the following action:
    i. Scores that fall between 61 and 79 percent call for **reinforcing** the skills taught in a particular Step.
    ii. Scores that fall below 60 percent indicate **reteaching** the content of that Step.
- See the section on "Using Student Performance for Instructional Planning" for more information about using the test scores.

Recording Content Mastery Test Scores

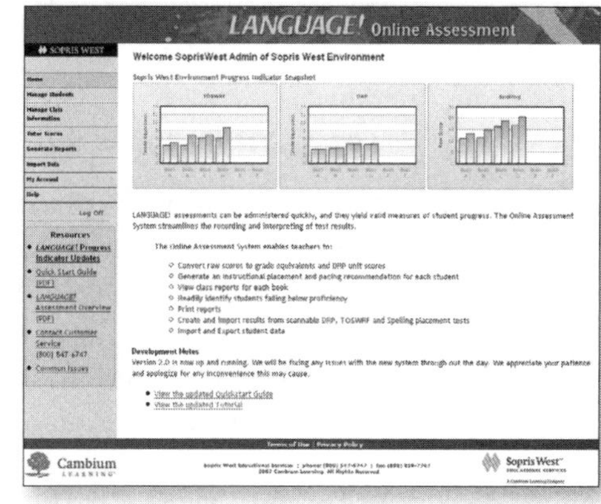

LANGUAGE! provides two options for recording and tracking Content Mastery scores:

1. Scores can be entered into the *Online Assessment System,* where student progress can be easily tracked.
2. Student scores can be recorded on the reproducible Content Mastery Task Class Roster that is provided for each book level in Appendix B. Teachers should prepare a roster for each unit of instruction.

Providing Feedback to Students

- Review answers for the Content Mastery tasks with students as recommended in the *Teacher Edition.* Use this as the starting point for reinforcement or reteaching of the content assessed on the test.
- Since the Content Mastery tasks show progress and are ongoing, remind students that their performance is an indicator of where their skills in literacy currently stand. Upcoming instruction will build on strengths and help improve areas of weakness identified by this test. Let students know that they will have multiple opportunities throughout the course of instruction to practice skills and work with content so that their scores on subsequent Content Mastery tasks improve. Students can compare their performance from one Content Mastery task to the next to see growth.

Ongoing Assessment

Using Student Performance Results for Instructional Planning

Using student scores to inform instruction:

- Patterns of performance by individual students or an entire class should inform teachers' instruction. *LANGUAGE!* offers built-in supports to address areas of weakness. A prescriptive teaching box follows each Content Mastery task. These boxes, which occur at the point of administration of the tests in the *Teacher Edition*, provide guidelines for reinforcing or reteaching content. They identify specific lessons, activities and technology tools to use within the unit. A sample appears below.

If...	Then...
Students score below 80%	**Reinforce:** • Word Meanings: Use *Sortegories*, Unit 9 • Use **Categorize It**, and **Sort It: Word Meanings**, Unit 9, Lesson 6, Step 3
Students score below 60%	**Reteach:** • Word Meanings: Use **Word Networks: Homophones**, Unit 9, Lesson 3, Step 3 • Use Multiple Meaning Map, Unit 9, Lesson 5, Step 3.

- In addition to the prescriptive teaching boxes, teachers can turn to the Special Instructional Support boxes positioned within the lessons for additional ideas for reinforcement.
- The teacher's examination of aggregated data for a class can suggest areas for additional instructional emphasis in subsequent units. For instance, if the data shows that most students scored below mastery on parts of speech, the teacher should place greater weight on this skill area as the class progresses through the remaining units of the book.

Retesting based on student performance:

- Once the appropriate measures have been taken to reinforce or reteach concepts based on student scores, it is advisable to retest students to ensure they are performing at 80% proficiency or above before moving on.
  - In the case of Steps 1 and 2, students will retake the same test with the same instruction being delivered from the *Teacher Edition*. Printable forms of those tests are available on the *Instructional Planning Tools* CD.
  - In the case of Steps 3 and 4, different forms of the test are provided which assess the same content, but with different items. Printable forms of these tests are available on the *Instructional Planning Tools* CD.
- If initial scores have been recorded in the *Online Assessment System*, the retest scores should be entered in the space that is provided.
- If the *Online Assessment System* is not used, enter the retest scores on the reproducible Content Mastery Task Class Roster that is provided for each book level in Appendix B. Use a different color or highlighter to identify the retest scores.

Moving to the next unit:

- Data from the Content Mastery tasks should inform instruction but not be an impediment to progressing through the curriculum in a timely manner. While the goal is having each student perform at 80 percent or better on these tasks, teachers can move to the next unit when 80 percent of the students have attained 80 percent of better on the Content Mastery tasks.
- Monitor closely the 20 percent of the students who didn't reach 80 percent. Scaffold instruction and provide extra practice for those students.

Comprehension Proficiency

Description

The *LANGUAGE!* curriculum provides two units in each book that contain Comprehension Proficiency tasks. Within those units, there are two lessons with specific tasks. In the first Comprehension Proficiency activity in the unit, teachers guide students through a series of multiple-choice questions. Instruction focuses on identifying signal words, question meaning, and examining distracter items. In the second activity in the unit, students are required to answer five multiple-choice questions on their own and write short answer responses.

Administering the Comprehension Proficiency Tasks

Unit lessons in the *Teacher Editions* provide the Comprehension Proficiency activities and the directions for using them. For each task, students use the Comprehension Proficiency exercises in the *Interactive Text*.

Scores and Their Interpretation

Each multiple-choice question has a possible correct score of five. Each open-ended question has a possible correct score of five. Teachers should use student performance information to fine tune emphasis on question signal words, which are the focus of the Answer It instructional activity in every unit, and on using the text selection to identify correct answers.

Benchmark Papers for Writing

Description

Benchmark Papers are part of the writing assessment component. These papers are written between the Baseline and end-of-book Progress Indicator writing samples to provide interim feedback to students on their writing performance. Benchmark Papers are not extra writing assignments; rather they are part of the ongoing curriculum. Because they are evaluated using the book-specific rubric, Benchmark Papers allow teachers to look at students' work in light of end-of-book expectations.

Administering the Benchmark Papers for Writing

Twice per book, there are designated writing assignments that will be used as Benchmark Papers. The *Teacher Editions* spell out the directions for the writing assignments—the prompt, the type of organizer, the type of written product required, and the use of the Writer's Checklist. Students use a graphic organizer or outline and write or word process their papers. Students are encouraged to use the Writer's Checklist, to revise and edit their papers. The Writer's Checklist is organized around the same Six Traits of Effective Writing as the book-specific rubric.

Scores and Their Interpretation

- Use the same trait-scoring approach to evaluate students' Benchmark Papers that is used to rate Progress Indicator writing samples. Judge each student's work in the context of the Six Traits of Effective Writing, assigning a rating of 4, 3, 2, or 1 for each of the traits.
- To rate the Benchmark Papers, duplicate the appropriate Writing Rubric from the *Instructional Planning Tools* CD. Attach a rubric to each student's writing sample.
- It is important to remember that the Six Traits of Effective Writing are not always distinct from one another. For instance, spelling performance in the Conventions category is easily classified as correct or incorrect and does not overlap in content with other traits. Voice and Audience Awareness, however, is more subjective and draws upon several traits. Therefore Voice and Audience Awareness is less easily rated.

- Rate the students' papers, using the appropriate rubric. Follow these steps:
    1. Read the student's work in its entirety once, without stopping. This provides a feel for the paper as a whole and permits a more accurate rating for Voice and Audience Awareness, a trait influenced by a number of factors.
    2. Reread the student's work, assigning a numerical score to each trait. Use a plus or minus in addition to the number if the student's work does not fit neatly into the description in a particular cell. Entering comments in the Teacher Comments may help explain the rating, but this is not a requirement.
    3. Transfer the points for each trait to the Writing: Rating Summary section in the student's *Summative Assessment* booklet.
    4. Enter the rating information into the *LANGUAGE! Online Assessment System* to maintain an electronic record of performance for analysis in guiding instruction or record all scores on the class roster found in Appendix B.

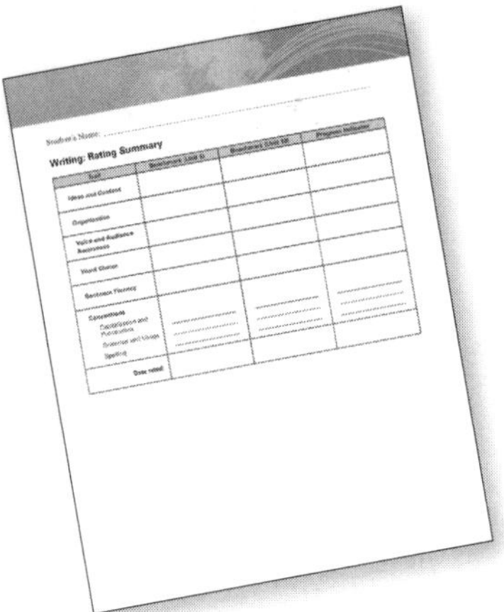

Providing Feedback to Students

When you have finished rating the Benchmark Papers, arrange to have a conference with each student about the rating of his or her paper. Have on hand the student's writing sample and the Writing: Rating Summary. It is also a good idea to have students refer to the Writer's Checklist to see how the rubric-based ratings relate to the checklist that they use. Focus students on their areas of strength and prompt them to verbalize their own improvement from paper to paper. On which traits has the student improved his or her performance? What areas still need work? Use this information to set writing goals with the student. You can also use this information to inform instruction in subsequent units.

Fluency

Description

Each unit provides multiple opportunities to monitor fluency proficiency. In each unit, students participate in designated fluency tasks for letter-sound, letter-name, word, phrase, and sentence fluency. Students work with peer partners to time each other, to keep track of errors, and to record fluency rates.

Administering the Fluency Tasks

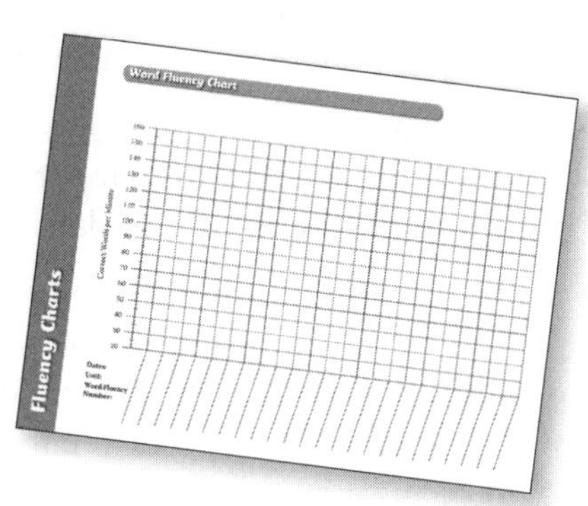

Each unit in the *Teacher Editions* for Books A–F contains Fluency tasks and the directions for administering them. For each task, students use the Fluency Charts in their *Interactive Text* to record and track their performance.

Interpreting Scores (WCPM)

The table below presents the recommended target number of words correct per minute (WCPM) for the end of each book in *LANGUAGE!*

LANGUAGE! Book Level	Target Number of Words Correct Per Minute
A	120
B	130
C	140
D	145
E	150
F	150–180

By the end of each book level, students should achieve a median (i.e., middle) or average score on two to three readings (of single words, sentences, or passages) relative to the book level WCPM. Given that older students typically read isolated words at a slower rate than connected text, expect that students' performance on Word Fluency may be lower than their performance on Sentence Fluency or Passage Fluency. If two or three scores fall below the target WCPM at the end of any book level, then an instructional change is needed.

Recording Fluency Rates

Fluency rates (i.e., number of letters or words read correctly per minute) for designated units should be entered into the *Online Assessment System.*

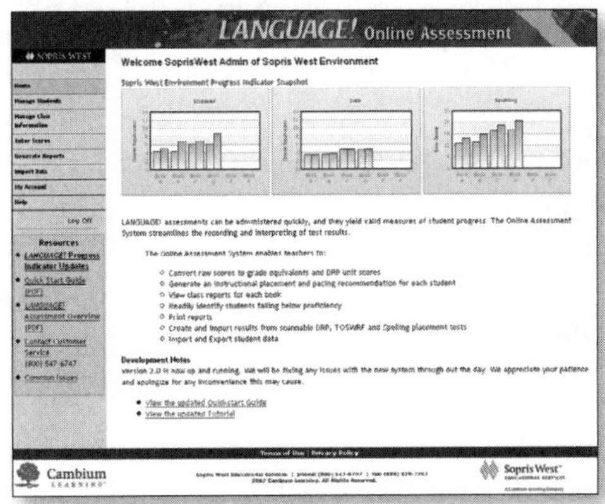

A time-saving approach to evaluate progress is to record students' performance on a limited set of results. The following Fluency tasks by book level are recommended:

Book A		Book B		Book C	
Fluency Task	When to Record Scores	Fluency Task	When to Record Scores	Fluency Task	When to Record Scores
• Word	Unit 2	• Word • Passage	Unit 9	• Word • Passage	Unit 15
• Word • Sentence	Unit 4	• Word • Passage	Unit 12	• Word • Passage	Unit 18
• Word • Sentence	Unit 6				

Book D		Book E		Book F	
Fluency Task	When to Record Scores	Fluency Task	When to Record Scores	Fluency Task	When to Record Scores
• Word • Passage	Unit 21	• Word • Passage	Unit 27	• Word • Passage	Unit 33
• Word • Passage	Unit 24	• Word • Passage	Unit 30	• Word • Passage	Unit 36

Setting Fluency Goals

Fluent word reading is important for comprehension; setting attainable goals is important to motivate a struggling reader. Given the importance of fluency for reading and motivation, it is essential to monitor fluency carefully and to set realistic goals. There are two situations for which setting interim or alternate fluency goals are beneficial.

- **Repeated Readings**

  Often students do not reach the target fluency rate on the first reading of a Word, Sentence or Passage Fluency in *LANGUAGE!* When this happens it is important to set an interim goal—a goal between the student's performance on the first reading and the target number of correct words per minute established for the book. To set the interim goal, take the words correct per minute (WCPM) and add 10 percent to that score.

  For example, in Book C the target WCPM is 140. If a student achieves 120 WCPM on the first reading of the Word Fluency 1 in a unit, the target WCPM on the student's fourth reading would be set at 132 (because 10% of 120 +12, and 120 + 12 = 132). The interim goal is 132 for the student rather than 140. If a student does not achieve this target after four readings, additional repeated readings of the same text with corrective feedback may be needed.

- **Modifying Fluency Goals for Students with Severe Reading Difficulties**

  If students beyond third grade have severe reading difficulties (i.e., performing more than two grade levels below grade level in reading), then use the following approach to set an alternate end-of-book goal:

  - Establish the student's median (i.e., middle) or average fluency score on two or three readings of the fluency tasks in the first unit of a book.

    For example, if a student working in Unit 13 scores 110 on Word Fluency 1, 106 on Word Fluency 2 and 115 on Word Fluency 3, the middle score (or median) is 110.

  - Set the interim fluency goal at 10 points above the median or average score.
  - In this example, the fluency goal for Word Fluency at the end of Book C would be set at 10 points above 110, which is 120 WCPM.

Using Student Performance Results for Instructional Planning

In addition to using student performance to set interim or alternative goals, teachers can use fluency data to inform areas of instruction that may require greater emphasis in subsequent units. For example, if students are making slow gains on Word Fluency tasks, be sure that individual sound-spelling correspondences are automatic and accurate.

End-of-Book Content Mastery

- Description
- Administration and Scoring Procedures
- Using End-of-Book Content Mastery for Exit Criteria
- Step 1: Phonemic Awareness and Phonics
- Step 3: Vocabulary and Morphology
- Step 4: Grammar and Usage

End-of-Book Content Mastery

Description

The End-of-Book Content Mastery for Book A consists of 50 multiple-choice and short-answer items. The test covers concepts, content, and skills presented in three major domains, or steps, in Book A:

- Step 1: Phonemic Awareness and Phonics
- Step 3: Vocabulary and Morphology
- Step 4: Grammar and Usage

Step 2, Step 5, and Step 6 are evaluated by Progress Indicators tests. Unlike the Content Mastery tasks, which are ongoing assessment measures used to give students immediate feedback and to adjust instruction, teachers administer the End-of-Book Content Mastery test to ascertain the extent to which students have acquired and can apply general concepts.

The table below presents the steps that are covered, the test sections within each step, focus of the questions, the number of items, and the format for each section for Book A.

Focus and Format of the End-of-Book Content Mastery Sections

Step	Test Section	Focus of Questions	Number of Items	Format
Step 1: Phonemic Awareness and Phonics	Word Study	Rhyme	5	Multiple-choice Teacher reads items
Step 3: Vocabulary and Morphology	Vocabulary	• Definitions based on categorization • Meaning based on context	10	Multiple-choice Teacher reads items (5) Student reads items (5)
	Word Relationships	Multiple meanings of words	5	Multiple-choice Teacher reads items
	Morphology	Correct usage of words with affixes	10	Multiple-choice (5) Short-answer (5) Student reads items
Step 4: Grammar and Usage	Grammar	Focus on grammar	10	Multiple-choice Student reads items
	Sentence Structure	Focus on sentence structure	10	

Administration and Scoring Procedures

Overall Directions

The End-of-Book Content Mastery test is to be administered at the end of six units of instruction (i.e., at the end of every Book, A to F) in the *LANGUAGE!* curriculum. So, in Book A, the End-of-Book Content Mastery is administered in Unit 6.

- Teachers should proceed from section to section without stopping for questions.
- The End-of-Book Content Mastery sections for Phonemic Awareness and Phonics, Vocabulary and Morphology, and Grammar and Usage are in a multiple-choice or short-answer format.
- Teachers should read the directions verbatim to ensure a standardized administration of the tests.

Scoring

The multiple-choice and short-answer sections, items 1–50, should be scored using the End-of-Book Content Mastery Answer Key—Book A.

Record of End-of-Book Content Mastery Scores

Enter student performance information in the *LANGUAGE! Online Assessment System.* Alternately, record scores on the reproducible End-of-Book Content Mastery Task Class Roster in Appendix B.

Interpreting the End-of-Book Content Mastery Results

Students' performance on the multiple-choice and short-answer sections can be used in two ways:

1. *Gauge overall performance:*
   The recommended overall performance standard is 80 percent (or 43/50 correct). That is, students should achieve 80 percent on the total test to pass and to demonstrate adequate progress toward reading outcomes.
2. *Look at student performance on each section of the test:*
   Students should achieve at least 80 percent (8/10 correct) on individual sections of the test. When performance falls below the 80 percent level on a section or sections, look closely at students' performance on the skills covered by that section(s). Patterns of unsatisfactory performance, such as a cluster of students falling below 80 percent on the same section(s), should be a signal for review and additional practice and/or reteaching before going on to the next book.

End-of-Book Content Mastery

Using End-of-Book Content Mastery for Exit Criteria

Performance on the End-of-Book Content Mastery is one of the components considered to determine if a student should exit from the *LANGUAGE!* curriculum. An overall score of 80% on the total test is recommended as one of the requirements for exiting. This level of content mastery, in conjunction with grade-level performance on the *LANGUAGE! Reading Scale*, are recommended in order to assure success with grade level curriculum requirements.

STEP 1

Phonemic Awareness and Phonics

Word Study

Have students turn to page 27 in their *Student Assessment* booklets. Check to be sure that students are on the correct page.

For this test, the teacher reads the test items out loud.

Say:

- Listen to the word.
- Then, listen to the word in a sentence, and possible rhyme choices for the word.
- Choose a rhyming word.
- Fill in the bubble for your choice.
- Look at the sample. (Read the sample out loud to students.)

Sample: *Listen:* fat.
The pig is a fat animal. Which word rhymes with fat? Fan, sat, fit, lit? fat

Ⓐ fan
Ⓑ sat (filled)
Ⓒ fit
Ⓓ lit

- Which bubble did you fill in? You should have filled in the bubble for the letter "B" for the word "sat." "Fat" rhymes with "sat."
- Continue to listen to the word, the sentence, and possible rhyme choices.
- Fill in the bubble for your answer.

1. *Listen:* quack.
The doctor was a quack.
Which word rhymes with quack? Quit, click, quick, sack? quack
Ⓐ quit
Ⓑ click
Ⓒ quick
Ⓓ sack (filled)

2. *Listen:* kick.
   The goal is to kick the ball.
   Which word rhymes with kick? Kid, lick, lack, sack? kick
   Ⓐ kid
   Ⓑ lick
   Ⓒ lack
   Ⓓ sack

3. *Listen:* hill.
   A hill is smaller than a mountain. Which word rhymes with hill? Will, lip, hit, hall? hill
   Ⓐ will
   Ⓑ lip
   Ⓒ hit
   Ⓓ hall

4. *Listen:* split.
   The man can split the log. Which word rhymes with split? Splat, glib, splint, grit? split
   Ⓐ splat
   Ⓑ glib
   Ⓒ splint
   Ⓓ grit

5. *Listen:* soft.
   The kitten's fur is soft. Which word rhymes with soft? Sift, gift, loft, golf? soft
   Ⓐ sift
   Ⓑ gift
   Ⓒ loft
   Ⓓ golf

STEP 3 Vocabulary and Morphology

Vocabulary Part A

Have students turn to page 28 in their *Student Assessment* booklets. Check to be sure that students are on the correct page.

For this test, the teacher reads the test items out loud.

Say:

- Look at the underlined words and possible meanings.
- Select the correct meaning for the underlined word and fill in the bubble for your answer.
- Look at the sample. (Read the sample out loud to students.)

> Sample: *Listen:* cat.
> Is cat an animal, a toy, clothing, an action, or a thing?
> cat
> (A) an animal
> (B) a toy
> (C) clothing
> (D) an action
> (E) a thing

- Which bubble did you fill in? You should have filled in the bubble for the letter "A" for "an animal." A cat is an animal.
- Look at and listen to these words and meanings.
- Fill in the bubble for your answer.

6. *Listen:* flick.
   Is flick a feeling, a person, a kind of music, an action, or an animal?
   flick
   (A) a feeling
   (B) a person
   (C) a plant
   (D) an action
   (E) an animal

7. *Listen:* sack.
   Is sack a container, furniture, a vehicle, a game, or an instrument?
   sack
   Ⓐ a container
   Ⓑ furniture
   Ⓒ a vehicle
   Ⓓ a game
   Ⓔ an instrument

8. *Listen:* fin.
   Is fin a part of a frog , a part of a pig, a part of a fish, a part of a plant, or a part of a van?
   fin
   Ⓐ a part of a frog
   Ⓑ a part of a pig
   Ⓒ a part of a fish
   Ⓓ a part of a plant
   Ⓔ a part of a van

9. *Listen:* sax.
   Is sax an animal, a person, a vehicle, a container, or an instrument?
   sax
   Ⓐ an animal
   Ⓑ a person
   Ⓒ a vehicle
   Ⓓ a container
   Ⓔ an instrument

10. *Listen:* crab.
    Is crab an animal from the desert, an animal from the jungle, an animal from the ocean, an animal from the hills, or an animal from the grasslands?
    crab
    Ⓐ an animal from the desert
    Ⓑ an animal from the jungle
    Ⓒ an animal from the ocean
    Ⓓ an animal from the hills
    Ⓔ an animal from the grasslands

Vocabulary Part B

Have students turn to page 29 in their *Student Assessment* booklets. Check to be sure that students are on the correct page.

For this test, students read the sentences on their own and the teacher reads the possible answers

Say:

- Read each sentence to yourself.
- Listen to the possible correct meanings for the underlined word in the sentence.
- Pick the correct meaning for the underlined word in the sentence.
- Fill in the bubble for your answer.
- Look at the sample. Read each sentence to yourself. (Do not read the sentence. Pause to allow students to read the sentence before reading the response options out loud; avoid pausing so long that the momentum of the test is disrupted.)

Sample:
Read the sentence: Rosa grabs her dad's bat for the picnic. (Teacher pauses)
Listen: In this sentence, does bat mean an animal, an action, a piece of sports equipment, or a plant? Fill in the bubble for your answer.

- Ⓐ an animal
- Ⓑ an action
- Ⓒ a piece of sports equipment (filled)
- Ⓓ a plant

- Which bubble did you fill in? You should have filled in the bubble for the letter "C" for "a piece of sports equipment." In this sentence, bat is a piece of sports equipment.
- Read each sentence.
- Then look at and listen to the possible meanings for the underlined word in the sentence.
- Fill in the bubble for your choice.

11. *Read:* Tim will fix the trim on the cabin.
Listen: In this sentence, does trim mean an action, an edge, a person who is fit, or a chair?
    - Ⓐ an action
    - Ⓑ an edge (filled)
    - Ⓒ a person who is fit
    - Ⓓ a chair

12. *Read:* A ram is a classic band mascot.
Listen: In this sentence, does ram mean an animal, a food, a car, or an action?
Ⓐ an animal
Ⓑ a food
Ⓒ a car
Ⓓ an action

13. *Read:* The bandit grabs the tin of jam.
Listen: In this sentence, does jam mean to play music in a band, to pack tightly, a kind of milk, or a kind of food?
Ⓐ to play music in a band
Ⓑ to pack tightly
Ⓒ a kind of milk
Ⓓ a kind of food

14. *Read:* The rabbit sniffs the mint on the blanket.
Listen: In this sentence, does mint mean something in perfect condition, a place where coins are made, a kind of food, or an action?
Ⓐ something in perfect condition
Ⓑ a place where coins are made
Ⓒ a kind of food
Ⓓ an action

15. *Read:* Jose will not hand Lin the toxic sandbag.
Listen: In this sentence, does hand mean a part of the body, to give, to drop, or a foot?
Ⓐ a part of the body
Ⓑ to give
Ⓒ to drop
Ⓓ a foot

Section 2
Word Relationships

Have students turn to page 30 in their *Student Assessment* booklets. Check to be sure that students are on the correct page.

In this test, the teacher reads the test items out loud.

Say:

- Look at and listen to the underlined word and possible meanings.
- Decide which is ***not*** one of the meanings for the underlined word. Fill in the bubble for your answer.
- Look at the sample. (Read the sample to students out loud.)

Sample: *Listen:* fan.
Which does not mean fan? A machine that blows air, a part of a fish, or a person who cheers for a team?
Ⓐ a machine that blows air
● (B) a part of a fish
Ⓒ a person who cheers for a team

- Which bubble did you fill in? You should have filled in the bubble for the letter "B" for "a part of a fish," because that is not a meaning of fan.
- Look at and listen to the words and possible meanings.
- Fill in the bubble for your answer.

16. *Listen:* bit.
Which does not mean bit? Something babies wear, a small piece of something, or a part of a horse's harness?
● (A) something babies wear
Ⓑ a small piece of something
Ⓒ a part of a horse's harness

17. *Listen:* hit.
Which does not mean hit? To make contact with something, a part of the body, or a successful movie or event?
Ⓐ to make contact with something
● (B) a part of the body
Ⓒ a successful movie or event

18. *Listen:* pick.
    Which does not mean pick? To select something, a farm animal, or a tool?
    Ⓐ to select something
    Ⓑ a farm animal
    Ⓒ a tool

19. *Listen:* jam.
    Which does not mean jam? Something eaten on bread, a difficult situation, or a hat?
    Ⓐ something eaten on bread
    Ⓑ a difficult situation
    Ⓒ a hat

20. *Listen:* lap.
    Which does not mean lap? A part of the body, to run around a field, or a place where a scientist works?
    Ⓐ a part of the body
    Ⓑ to run around a field
    Ⓒ a place where a scientist works

Morphology Part A

Have students turn to page 31 in their *Student Assessment* booklets. Check to be sure that students are on the correct page.

For this test, students read the test items on their own.

Say:

- Read each sentence on your own.
- One of the words below the sentence correctly completes it.
- Read the possible answers.
- Fill in the bubble for the word that correctly completes the sentence.
- Look at the sample. Read the sentence and possible answers. Fill in the bubble for your answer. (Do not read the sample or test items out loud. Do not read the sentences or the possible answers. Give students time to do the sample by themselves.)

Sample: The _______ were in the back of the van.
Ⓐ bat
Ⓑ bags
Ⓒ bag
Ⓓ bag's

- Which bubble did you fill in? You should have filled in the bubble for the letter "B" for "bags." "Bags" correctly completes the sentence: The bags were in the back of the van.
- Read the sentences and possible choices on your own.
- Fill in the bubble for your answer.

21. Al and Kim have big back _______.
    - Ⓐ pack
    - Ⓑ packs
    - Ⓒ pals
    - Ⓓ pack's

22. Toxins sink into a _______ skin.
    - Ⓐ frog
    - Ⓑ frogs
    - Ⓒ frog's
    - Ⓓ frogs'

23. The _______ of the fish are big.
    - Ⓐ gill
    - Ⓑ gills
    - Ⓒ gill's
    - Ⓓ gills'

24. The polluted air can make _______ sick.
    - Ⓐ plant
    - Ⓑ plants
    - Ⓒ plant's
    - Ⓓ plants'

25. _______ glasses are lost.
    - Ⓐ Ben
    - Ⓑ Bens
    - Ⓒ Bens'
    - Ⓓ Ben's

Morphology Part B

Have students turn to page 32 in their *Student Assessment* booklets. Check to be sure that students are on the correct page.

For this test, students read the test items on their own.

Say:

- Read the verb in the left column.
- Then read the sentence in the middle column. The sentence has a blank. Change the verb into the present tense to fit the sentence. Write it in the blank.
- Read the sentence in the right column. It also has a blank. Change the verb into the present progressive to fit the sentence. Write it in the blank.
- Read the verb in the sample. Rewrite the verb into the present tense to match the sentence in the middle column. Then rewrite the verb into the present progressive to match the sentence in the right column. (Do not read the sample or test items out loud. Give students time to do the sample by themselves. You may read the column labels to students.)

Sample:

Verb	Present Tense	Present Progressive
mop	She __mops__ the spill with a paper towel.	I __am mopping__ the spill with a paper towel.

- What are the words you wrote in the blanks?
- For present tense in the middle column, you should have written mops, because mops is the present tense verb in the sentence: She mops the spill with a wig.
- For present progressive in the right column, you should have written: am mopping, because am mopping is the present progressive in the sentence: I am mopping the spill with a wig.

- Read each verb in the left column.
- Rewrite the verb into the present tense in the middle column. Then rewrite the verb into the present progressive in the right column.
- Make sure to match the verb with the subject in each sentence.

Verb	Present Tense	Present Progressive
26. stop	The quick cop __stops__ traffic.	The quick cops __are stopping__ traffic.
27. spill	Those vans __spill__ globs of toxin.	Which van __is spilling__ globs of toxins?
28. drift	Black fog __drifts__ from the toxic spot.	Black fog __is drifting__ from the toxic spot.
29. sniff	The man __sniffs__ at the black fog.	The men __are sniffing__ at the black fog.
30. plan	We __plan__ to block toxic vans.	I __am planning__ to block toxic vans.

STEP

Grammar and Usage

Section 1
Grammar

Have students turn to page 33 in their *Student Assessment* booklets. Check to be sure that students are on the correct page.

For this test, students read the test items on their own.

Say:

- Read each sentence.
- Then read the parts of speech below the sentence.
- Decide which part of speech best describes the underlined word or group of words in the sentence. The answer could be: a singular noun, a plural noun, a possessive noun, a third person singular present tense verb, a present progressive verb, a direct object, an adverb, or an adjective.
- Fill in the bubble for your answer.
- Read the sample and fill in the bubble next to the correct answer. (Do not read the sample or test items out loud. Give students time to do the sample by themselves. You may help students read the response options.)

Sample: The van is big.
- Ⓐ an adjective
- Ⓑ a direct object
- Ⓒ a singular noun (filled)
- Ⓓ a present progressive tense verb
- Ⓔ an adverb

- Which bubble did you fill in? You should have filled in the bubble for the letter "C" for "singular noun," because **van** is a singular noun.
- Continue to read the sentences and the possible answers. Decide which answer best describes the underlined word or words.
- Fill in the bubble for your answer.

31. The frog flops like a fish on land.
- Ⓐ a plural noun
- Ⓑ an adverb
- Ⓒ a direct object
- Ⓓ a present progressive verb
- Ⓔ a third person singular present tense verb (filled)

32. The bandit hid the toxic pill.
    - Ⓐ an adjective
    - Ⓑ a direct object
    - Ⓒ a singular noun
    - Ⓓ a present progressive verb
    - Ⓔ an adverb

33. Don is swimming from the raft to the dock.
    - Ⓐ a possessive noun
    - Ⓑ a direct object
    - Ⓒ a third person singular present tense verb
    - Ⓓ a present progressive verb
    - Ⓔ an adjective

34. Luna spills water on Kim's deformed frog.
    - Ⓐ an adjective
    - Ⓑ a possessive noun
    - Ⓒ a direct object
    - Ⓓ a plural noun
    - Ⓔ an adverb

35. The pond's water was toxic from gas spilled from the gas pump.
    - Ⓐ an adjective
    - Ⓑ a possessive noun
    - Ⓒ a direct object
    - Ⓓ a plural noun
    - Ⓔ an adverb

36. The clinic's staff had a snack.
    - Ⓐ an adjective
    - Ⓑ a possessive noun
    - Ⓒ a direct object
    - Ⓓ a singular noun
    - Ⓔ an adverb

37. If polluted air drifts in, my dog gets ill.
    - Ⓐ an adjective
    - Ⓑ a possessive noun
    - Ⓒ a direct object
    - Ⓓ a singular noun
    - Ⓔ an adverb

38. The mascot is yapping like a sick duck.
   Ⓐ an adjective
   Ⓑ a possessive noun
   Ⓒ a direct object
   Ⓓ a singular noun
   Ⓔ a third person singular present tense verb

39. Pesticide run-off is quickly spilling into our lakes.
   Ⓐ an adjective
   Ⓑ a third person singular present tense verb
   Ⓒ a direct object
   Ⓓ a present progressive verb
   Ⓔ an adverb

40. The cops plod down the hill and across the rocks to the pond.
   Ⓐ an adjective
   Ⓑ a plural noun
   Ⓒ a singular noun
   Ⓓ a possessive noun
   Ⓔ an adverb

Section 2
Sentence Structure Part A

Have students turn to page 35 in their *Student Assessment* booklets. Check to be sure that students are on the correct page.

For this test, students read the test items on their own.

Say:

- Read each sentence on your own.
- Which word or group of words make up the subject?
- Read the possible answers.
- Fill in the bubble for the word or group of words that is the subject. (Do not read the sentences or response options out loud. Give students time to do items 41–45 by themselves.)

41. Ron's dad quits his toxic habits.
   Ⓐ toxic habits
   Ⓑ dad
   Ⓒ quits
   Ⓓ habits
   Ⓔ quits his toxic habits

42. The lap dog can lick the snacks.
    - Ⓐ can lick the snacks
    - Ⓑ dog
    - Ⓒ lick
    - Ⓓ snacks
    - Ⓔ can lick

43. The ill child grabs the napkins from the box.
    - Ⓐ child
    - Ⓑ napkins
    - Ⓒ grabs the napkins from the box
    - Ⓓ grabs
    - Ⓔ from the box

44. Black fog drifts quickly from the toxic spot.
    - Ⓐ drifts quickly from the toxic spot
    - Ⓑ toxic spot
    - Ⓒ drifts
    - Ⓓ fog
    - Ⓔ drifts quickly

45. I mop the spill with a quilt.
    - Ⓐ mop the spill with a quilt
    - Ⓑ with a quilt
    - Ⓒ the spill
    - Ⓓ I mop
    - Ⓔ I

Sentence Structure Part B

Have students turn to page 36 in their *Student Assessment* booklets. Check to be sure that students are on the correct page.

For this test, students read the test items on their own.

Say:

- Read each sentence on your own.
- Which word or group of words make up the predicate?
- Read the possible answers.
- Fill in the bubble for the word or group of words that is the predicate.
  (Do not read the sentences or response options out loud. Give students time to do items 46–50 by themselves.)

46. The black ducks quack on the pond.
    - Ⓐ ducks
    - Ⓑ on the pond
    - Ⓒ black ducks
    - Ⓓ black ducks quack
    - Ⓔ quack (filled)

47. The jock is sliding to the backstop.
    - Ⓐ is
    - Ⓑ is sliding (filled)
    - Ⓒ jock
    - Ⓓ sliding
    - Ⓔ backstop

48. The inn profits from our jazz band.
    - Ⓐ inn
    - Ⓑ jazz band
    - Ⓒ inn profits
    - Ⓓ from our jazz band
    - Ⓔ profits (filled)

49. Ken and Jan split a nonfat hot dog.
    - Ⓐ split (filled)
    - Ⓑ Ken and Jan
    - Ⓒ nonfat hot dog
    - Ⓓ hot dog
    - Ⓔ Ken and Jan split

50. The lost dogs are zigzagging across the land.
    - Ⓐ across the land
    - Ⓑ dogs
    - Ⓒ are zigzagging (filled)
    - Ⓓ zigzagging
    - Ⓔ are

End-of-Book Content Mastery

Answer Key—Book A

S.	Ⓐ	●	Ⓒ	Ⓓ
1.	Ⓐ	Ⓑ	Ⓒ	●
2.	Ⓐ	●	Ⓒ	Ⓓ
3.	●	Ⓑ	Ⓒ	Ⓓ
4.	Ⓐ	Ⓑ	Ⓒ	●
5.	Ⓐ	Ⓑ	●	Ⓓ

S.	●	Ⓑ	Ⓒ	Ⓓ	Ⓔ
6.	Ⓐ	Ⓑ	Ⓒ	●	Ⓔ
7.	●	Ⓑ	Ⓒ	Ⓓ	Ⓔ
8.	Ⓐ	Ⓑ	●	Ⓓ	Ⓔ
9.	Ⓐ	Ⓑ	Ⓒ	Ⓓ	●
10.	Ⓐ	Ⓑ	●	Ⓓ	Ⓔ

S.	Ⓐ	Ⓑ	●	Ⓓ
11.	Ⓐ	●	Ⓒ	Ⓓ
12.	●	Ⓑ	Ⓒ	Ⓓ
13.	Ⓐ	Ⓑ	Ⓒ	●
14.	Ⓐ	Ⓑ	●	Ⓓ
15.	Ⓐ	●	Ⓒ	Ⓓ

S.	Ⓐ	●	Ⓒ
16.	●	Ⓑ	Ⓒ
17.	Ⓐ	●	Ⓒ
18.	Ⓐ	●	Ⓒ
19.	Ⓐ	Ⓑ	●
20.	Ⓐ	Ⓑ	●

S.	Ⓐ	●	Ⓒ	Ⓓ
21.	Ⓐ	●	Ⓒ	Ⓓ
22.	Ⓐ	Ⓑ	●	Ⓓ
23.	Ⓐ	●	Ⓒ	Ⓓ
24.	Ⓐ	●	Ⓒ	Ⓓ
25.	Ⓐ	Ⓑ	Ⓒ	●

Give one point for each item 26–30 only if both answers are correct (present tense and present progressive).

S.	mops	am mopping
26.	stops	are stopping
27.	spill	is spilling
28.	drifts	is drifting
29.	sniffs	are sniffing
30.	plan	am planning

S.	Ⓐ	Ⓑ	●	Ⓓ	Ⓔ
31.	Ⓐ	Ⓑ	Ⓒ	Ⓓ	●
32.	●	Ⓑ	Ⓒ	Ⓓ	Ⓔ
33.	Ⓐ	Ⓑ	Ⓒ	●	Ⓔ
34.	Ⓐ	●	Ⓒ	Ⓓ	Ⓔ
35.	Ⓐ	●	Ⓒ	Ⓓ	Ⓔ
36.	Ⓐ	Ⓑ	●	Ⓓ	Ⓔ
37.	●	Ⓑ	Ⓒ	Ⓓ	Ⓔ
38.	Ⓐ	Ⓑ	Ⓒ	●	Ⓔ
39.	Ⓐ	Ⓑ	Ⓒ	Ⓓ	●
40.	Ⓐ	●	Ⓒ	Ⓓ	Ⓔ

41.	Ⓐ	●	Ⓒ	Ⓓ	Ⓔ
42.	Ⓐ	●	Ⓒ	Ⓓ	Ⓔ
43.	●	Ⓑ	Ⓒ	Ⓓ	Ⓔ
44.	Ⓐ	Ⓑ	Ⓒ	●	Ⓔ
45.	Ⓐ	Ⓑ	Ⓒ	Ⓓ	●

46.	Ⓐ	Ⓑ	Ⓒ	Ⓓ	●
47.	Ⓐ	●	Ⓒ	Ⓓ	Ⓔ
48.	Ⓐ	Ⓑ	Ⓒ	Ⓓ	●
49.	●	Ⓑ	Ⓒ	Ⓓ	Ⓔ
50.	Ⓐ	Ⓑ	●	Ⓓ	Ⓔ

Baseline Assessments and Progress Indicators

- Test of Silent Contextual Reading Fluency (TOSCRF)
- The *LANGUAGE!* Reading Scale (LRS)
- Test of Written Spelling (TWS-4)
- Writing

Test of Silent Contextual Reading Fluency (TOSCRF)

Description of the TOSCRF

The Test of Silent Contextual Reading Fluency (TOSCRF) measures the speed with which students can recognize the individual words in a series of printed passages that become progressively more difficult in their content, vocabulary, and grammar.

The TOSCRF is primarily a measure of silent contextual reading fluency. Because TOSCRF scores reflect competence in so many aspects of reading (e.g., word identification, comprehension, fluency), they can be used to estimate general reading ability and to identify both good and poor readers.

The TOSCRF measures a wide variety of essential interrelated silent reading skills, including the ability to do the following:

- Recognize printed words and know their meaning
- Use one's mastery of syntax and morphology (i.e., grammar) to facilitate understanding the meaning of written sentences and passages
- Incorporate word knowledge and grammar knowledge to quickly grasp the meaning of words, sentences, paragraphs, stories, newspapers, novels, and poetry—in short, all contextual material
- Read and understand contextual material at a pace fast enough to make silent reading practical and enjoyable

Because the test assesses so many abilities that are essential to fluent reading, its results are impressive and extraordinarily accurate measures of reading competence and, therefore, can be used confidently to identify both poor and good readers. Evidence for these claims is found in Chapters 5 and 6 of the TOSCRF Examiner's Manual (Hammill, Wiederholt, and Allen, 2006) which deal with reliability and validity, respectively.

The test was normed on a nationally representative sample of 1,898 students, ranging in age from 7 years 0 months to 18 years 11 months, each of whom was administered all four forms of the TOSCRF. These students resided in 23 states. The test provides raw scores, standard scores, percentiles, and grade equivalents.

The passages that the students are given to read are adapted from passages in the Gray Oral Reading Tests–Fourth Edition (Wiederholt & Bryant, 2001) and the Gray Silent Reading Tests (Wiederholt & Blalock, 2000). The easy passages use preprimer- and first-grade-level words and simple grammar; the difficult passages use adult-level words and complex grammar (embedded phrases, sequenced adjectives, affixes, etc.). The passages are printed in uppercase without punctuation or spaces between the words, as shown in this example:

AYELLOWBIRDWITHBLUEWINGSSATONMOTHERSPRETTYHAT

Students are given 3 minutes to draw lines between as many words as possible, as follows:

A|YELLOW|BIRD|WITH|BLUE|WINGS|SAT|ON|MOTHERS|PRETTY|HAT

Each form can be administered to one student or to an entire classroom of students in approximately 10 minutes, including the time necessary for explaining the directions and completing the practice items.

Readers interested in specific details pertaining to norming and validity and reliability results for the TOSCRF should see the TOSCRF Examiner's Manual (Hammill, Wiederholt, and Allen, 2006).

Administration and Scoring Procedures

This section contains information dealing with how to administer and score the TOSCRF.

Included is information concerning who is competent to administer, score, and interpret the TOSCRF, who should be tested, and specific administration and scoring instructions.

Basic Testing Procedure

The chart below shows the TOSCRF Form (A and B) for Baseline and Progress Indicator assessments.

	Baseline	Progress Indicator
Test Form	Student *Baseline and Summative Assessment* booklet, Form A, page 4	Student *Baseline and Summative Assessment* booklet, Form B, page 37
When to administer	Before Unit 1	Unit 6

Individuals who are administering the TOSCRF for the first time should:

1. Study the content of this section carefully.
2. Practice administering the test until they become comfortable with the test's unique features.
3. In order to ensure a uniform administration across all students who take these tests, it is very important that you read aloud **WORD FOR WORD** the bolded text that follows the word "SAY." The material in italic is information for you and should not be read to the students.
4. Allow approximately 10 minutes to administer the TOSCRF, including the time necessary for explaining the directions and completing the practice items, to one student or to an entire classroom of students.

Most professionals can score the TOSCRF, using the Scoring Keys on page 72 for Baseline Form A and on page 74 for Progress Indicator Form B, provided they:

(a) have thoroughly read this manual and/or received special inservice training on scoring this test and

(b) have scored correctly the 10 example Student Record Forms provided in Appendix A. The example forms in Appendix A are provided to ensure standardized scoring of the TOSCRF. The correct answers for the example forms can be found at the end of Appendix A (see Table A.1). *Professionals must not attempt to score the TOSCRF until their scoring of the practice Student Record Forms equals the scoring provided in Appendix A.* Questions concerning why a particular example item was scored a certain way can be answered by reviewing the scoring instructions provided later in this chapter.

Whoever interprets the TOSCRF scores should have a basic understanding of testing statistics and knowledge of the general procedures governing test administration, scoring, and interpretation.

Eligibility Criteria

The TOSCRF may be used to measure the reading skills of most students between the ages of 7-0 and 18-11 (Grades 2 through 12). The TOSCRF should not be administered to students younger than 7-0 or older than 18-11. Only students who understand the directions and can formulate the necessary responses should be given this test.

Specific Administration Instructions

To administer the TOSCRF for Book A, examiners will need a TOSCRF Student Record Form, found in the student *Baseline and Summative Assessment* booklet, and a stopwatch or a watch or clock with a second hand. Each student will need a sharp pencil or a ballpoint pen.

Students are allowed exactly 3 minutes on each form (the entire testing session should take approximately 10 minutes). This test can be administered to entire classes, to small groups, or to individual students (e.g., to a student receiving remedial instruction or to a special education student). The same instructions are used for all forms.

The two example items are provided to teach the students how to take the test and how to self-correct.

The Practice Form on page 5 for Form A (Baseline) or page 38 for Form B (Progress Indicator) gives students an opportunity to become familiar with marking the test's passages quickly and accurately. Be sure that students correctly complete Example 2. You may double-check students' understanding of the task by checking their work on the Practice Form.

When testing individuals, discontinue testing if the student fails to correctly identify the example words or if the student has any problems using a pen or pencil. When testing groups, allow all students to attempt the test, even those who fail the example items and Practice Form.

Group Administration

<u>**Step 1:**</u>

Before testing begins, turn to page 4 for Form A (Baseline) or page 37 for Form B (Progress Indicator) in the student Baseline and Summative Assessment *booklet. Print the two example rows shown on the Student Record Form on a chalkboard, dry erase board, or overhead projector so that they are clearly visible to the students being tested.*

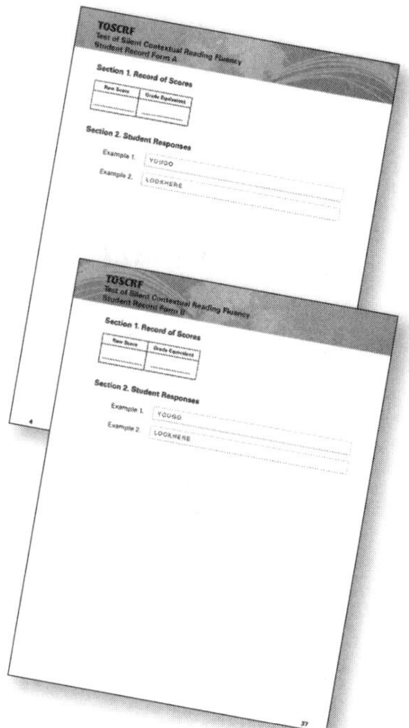

<u>**Step 2:**</u>

Have students turn to page 4 for Baseline or page 37 for Progress Indicator in their Baseline and Summative Assessment *booklets. Check to see that students are on the correct page.*

<u>**Step 3:**</u>

SAY:

- **Do not turn the page until I tell you to.**

Once all students have opened to the correct page:

SAY:

- **Look at the first row of words labeled Example 1 at the bottom of the page.**

Hold up a student booklet for the class to see and point to the first row labeled "Example 1", then refer to the example rows printed on the board.

SAY:

- **See how the words in this sentence are run together? If you draw a line between *you* and *go*, you will have a sentence that reads "You go."**

Demonstrate this with the example printed on the board.

YOU|GO

SAY:

- **Notice that I don't draw a line at the beginning of the row or at the end of the row. If you make a mistake while you're working and draw the line in the wrong place, don't try to erase it. Just draw a line through the top of the wrong line and draw a new line where you think it should go.**

Demonstrate this on the board by placing a mark in the middle of a word and then correcting it.

YO|U|GO

SAY:

- **Now look at Example 2. The words in this sentence also have been run together. You find the two words that make this sentence. Each time you find a word in the sentence, draw a line after it.** *(Wait for the students to respond.)* **Did you find the words *look* and *here*?**

Check the work of each student being tested. Instruct students who do not understand the task until they completely understand the task. If they fail to understand, have them attempt to take the test with the other students but do not score their tests.

Once the students have completed the examples successfully:

SAY:

- **Now I want you to do some more sentences like the ones you just did. When I say "go," turn the page in your booklet and begin. You'll have 2 minutes to find the words in as many sentences as you can.**

(Turn the page in a student's booklet and show the Practice Form.)

SAY:

- **Work as fast as you can without making mistakes. When I say "begin," start here with passage A** *(point to Passage A)* **and keep going until you reach the end of the row. When you complete a row, go to the next one. When you complete a passage, go to the next one. Don't skip any rows or passages, and don't draw a line at the beginning or end of a row. You will start at the top of the page and keep going until I say "stop" or until you see a stop sign at the bottom of the page.**
- **Remember, if you draw a line in the wrong place, just make a cross through the top of the wrong line and put a new line where you think it should go. If you draw the line in the right place, a real word will be on each side of the line with no extra letters between them and the line will be between two words that make sense in the sentence. If you don't see a word you know, keep going until you do see a word you know.**
- **Now, turn the page. It should say "Practice Form" at the top of the page.** *(Pause.)* **Begin.** *Begin timing. After exactly 2 minutes, say,* **Stop**.

Monitor the students' work to be sure everyone understands the task. When you are sure they all understand how to take the test:

SAY:

- **This time you'll have 3 minutes to find all the words in as many sentences as you can. When I say "begin," turn the page in your booklet and work as fast as you can without making mistakes. When you get to the bottom of the page, go to the next page and keep working until I say "stop" or you come to the stop sign at the end of the test. Now turn the page.** *(Pause.)* **Begin.**

After exactly 3 minutes:

SAY:

- **Stop.**

Individual Administration

Use the same instructions for individual administration as the ones for group administration. However, instead of writing the examples on the board, point to and demonstrate the examples in the student's assessment booklet.

If it is evident that the student cannot, for whatever reason, perform the task, stop testing.

Scoring the TOSCRF

Scoring the TOSCRF is quick and easy. Before scoring, make sure that every student has truly attempted to identify the words on the Practice Form. Examiners can usually tell when students do not understand the task or, due to lack of motivation, do not make a sincere effort to correctly identify the words in each passage.

FATHER|WENT|OUT|TO|BUY|SOME|PRETTY|FLOWERS|THE|CAKE
COOKED|A|LITTLE|TOO|LONG|SO|IT|WAS|BROWN

Figure 4.1

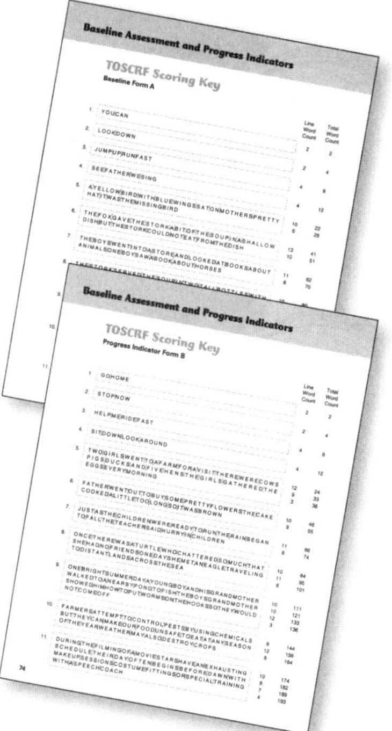

If the student successfully completed the example words and demonstrated understanding of the task on the Practice Form, begin scoring with the last row that the student attempted. Score backwards until you reach the point at which the student has correctly identified all of the words in one passage or until all words have been scored. A word is correctly identified when a line is clearly drawn separating the word from another word. Disregard any lines drawn before the first word or after the last word on a row. Figure 4.1 demonstrates a passage in which every word is correctly identified.

The student receives credit for all the words from Passage 1 to the completely correct passage and is awarded 1 point for each word correctly identified after that correct passage. When a student does not identify all the words correctly in any of the attempted passages, the total TOSCRF raw score is the total number of correctly identified words.

The scoring keys for the TOSCRF are provided on pages 72–73 for Form A (Baseline) and pages 74–75 for Form B (Progress Indicator).

For your convenience, the scoring keys provide the word count for each row and the cumulative word count on the far right of each page. Appendix A provides 10 scored examples for practice. Before attempting to score the test, practice scoring the 10 examples provided in Appendix A. The correct scores are provided in Table A.1 at the end of Appendix A. Compare your scores with the correct scores provided in that section. Do not attempt to score an actual test until your scores match the correct scores.

Eventually, you will encounter some scoring issues. Several common scoring problems to look out for are skipped rows, misplaced lines, and self-corrections.

Skipped Rows

Before scoring the TOSCRF, look to see if the student skipped any rows. If the student has skipped a row, do not score the test. Instead, retest the student using an alternate form of the TOSCRF.

Misplaced Lines

A line may be partially drawn over a letter to the extent that more of the letter appears on the side of the letter closest to the letters that constitute the word. In Figure 4.2, although the line is partially drawn over the letter *g* in *gave*, most of the letter is visible on the side nearest the letters that make up the word. Therefore, the student should receive credit for both *fox* and *gave*. This row would receive a score of 13 points.

THE|FOX|GAVE|THE|STORK|A|BIT|OF|THE|SOUP|IN|A|SHALLOW
DISH|BUT|THE|STORK|COULD|NOT|EAT|FROM|THE|DISH

Figure 4.2

If a line is drawn over a letter so that less of the letter is visible on the side closest to the letters that constitute the word, both the word in question and the adjacent word are scored incorrect (see Figure 4.3). Because less of the letters *b* and *s* are visible on the correct side (i.e., closest to the letters that make up the word), this student would not get credit for the words *at, books,* or *about.* This row receives a score of 7 points. Similarly, because the student's line is drawn directly over the middle of the letter *o* in the word *one* on the second row, no credit is given for either *animals* or *one.* This row receives a score of 4 points.

THE|BOYS|WENT|INTO|A|STORE|AND|LOOKED|AT|BOOK|SABOUT
ANIMALS|ONE|BOY|SAW|A|BOOK|ABOUT|HORSES

Figure 4.3

Sometimes a student fails to draw a line that fully separates two words. When this happens, the score is based on where the line would extend if it were fully drawn. In Figure 4.4, *just* and *as* are not credited because an extension of the first line would make this line incorrect. However, *the* is credited because the extension of the third line would be correct. This row would receive a score of 5 points. (Note that credit is not given for *children, were, ready,* or *to* because the line was drawn directly over the middle of the letters *n* and *y.*)

JUS|TAS|THE|CHILDRE/NWERE|READ|YTO|RUN|THE|RAIN|BEGAN
TO|FALL|THE|TEACHER|SAID|HURRY|IN|CHILDREN

Figure 4.4

If the student draws a line with a strong right or left slant, the word is considered correct provided the line does not extend more than halfway above or below the midpoint of the letter on the correct side of the letter. In the first row in Figure 4.4, the student should be credited for *the* but should not be credited for *children* or *were.*

Self-Corrections

Although the students are told to self-correct in a particular manner, accept any self-correction if the student's intent is clearly evident. Figure 4.5 shows the proper method of self-correction between the words *of* and *the*. The self-corrections in the words *into*, *backyard*, and *she* should also be credited. However, the self-correction between *little* and *pet* is unclear; therefore, both words should be scored as incorrect.

A|GIRL|RAN|OUT|OF|THE|WHITE|HOUSE|INTO|THE|BACKYARD
MOTHER|SHE|SAID|MY|LITTLE|PET|BIRD|IS|GONE

Figure 4.5

Interpreting TOSCRF Results

In this section, we discuss how to record, analyze, and use the TOSCRF results.

Topics include (a) how to record the scores, (b) how to interpret the various types of scores yielded by the test, (c) using student performance results for instructional planning, and (d) how to evaluate growth.

Recording of TOSCRF Scores

Converting raw scores to normative scores can happen in two ways: manually or by using the *Online Assessment System*. The *Online Assessment System* provides users with the normative scores listed in the table below. Without use of the *Online Assessment System* (manual recording of scores), only grade equivalents are provided.

Normative Scores Provided	
Online Assessment System	Manual
Converts raw scores to: • grade equivalents • percentile ranks • standard scores • descriptive ratings of standard scores	Converts raw scores to: • grade equivalents
Note: no need to use print record forms	**Note:** must use print record forms: TOSCRF Student Record Form, Summary Record Form, Baseline and Progress Indicator Class Roster.

Recording Using the *LANGUAGE! Online Assessment System*

Enter raw scores into the *LANGUAGE! Online Assessment System*. The Web-based data entry and reporting system will convert raw scores to percentile ranks and standard scores, grade equivalents, and descriptive ratings of the tests' standard scores. Student birth date and test date must be entered in the *Online Assessment System* to obtain standard scores and percentiles.

Detailed discussions of the normative scores are found in the "Test Scores and Their Interpretation" section of this chapter. The descriptive ratings of the standard scores are found in Table 4.1.

Manual Recording

Use the conversion table on page 76 to convert TOSCRF raw scores to grade equivalents. A detailed discussion of grade equivalents is found in the next section "Test Scores and Their Interpretation".

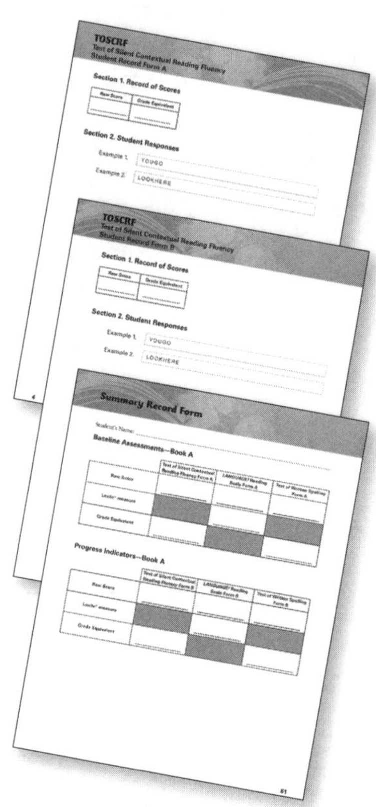

Once grade equivalents are obtained, scores should be recorded on the print record forms:

- **TOSCRF Student Record Form** – An individual's test performance is recorded on the TOSCRF's Student Record Form in the student *Baseline and Summative Assessment* on page 4 for Baseline Form A and page 37 for Progress Indicator Form B.
- **Summary Record Form** – This form summarizes all Baseline and Summative Assessment scores for an individual. This form can be found in the student *Baseline and Summative Assessment,* on page 61.
- **Baseline and Progress Indicator Class Roster** – This form summarizes all Baseline and Progress Indicator assessment scores (not including writing) for a class. Transfer scores from the students' Summary Record Forms to the Baseline and Progress Indicator Class Roster found in Appendix B.

Test Scores and Their Interpretation

The chart below shows the normative scores provided for TOSCRF: raw scores, standard scores, percentile ranks, and grade equivalents. This section includes a brief discussion of each score and how it should be interpreted. The shortcomings of these scores and cautions about their use are also discussed.

Normative Scores Provided	
Online Assessment System	Manual
Converts raw scores to: • grade equivalents • percentile ranks • standard scores • descriptive ratings of standard scores	Converts raw scores to: • grade equivalents

Raw Scores

The TOSCRF raw score is the total number of words correctly identified. These scores are useful only for generating normative scores, such as standard scores, percentiles, and grade equivalents.

Standard Scores

The clearest indication of a student's performance on the TOSCRF is provided by a standard score. This type of score provides a precise estimate of how far a student's score is from the average of other students from the normative sample at the same age. It can be used to compare performance on TOSCRF with performance on the Test of Written Spelling (TWS). Lyman (1998) defined a standard score as "any of several derived scores based on the number of standard deviations between a given raw score and the mean of the distribution" (p. 160). The standard scores on the TOSCRF are derived from a distribution that has a mean of 100 and a standard deviation of 15. This distribution was chosen because it is already well known to examiners who use the *Wechsler Intelligence Scale for Children–Fourth Edition* (Wechsler, 2003), the *Woodcock–Johnson III* (Woodcock, McGrew, & Mather, 2001), the *Test of Word Reading Efficiency* (Torgesen, Wagner, & Rashotte, 1999), the *Test of Silent Word Reading Fluency* (Mather, Hammill, Allen, & Roberts, 2004), and many other popular tests of aptitude, language, and achievement. Guidelines for interpreting standard scores are provided in Table 4.1.

Raw scores are converted to standard scores using the *LANGUAGE! Online Assessment System.* To obtain standard scores, raw scores along with the date on which the student was tested and birth date must be entered into the *LANGUAGE! Online Assessment System.*

Readers interested in specific details about the development of the TOSCRF standard scores should see the TOSCRF Examiner's Manual (Hammill, Wiederholt, and Allen, 2006).

Professionals who develop, review, and use tests have become increasingly concerned about floor and ceiling effects in diagnostic and screening measures. Bracken (1987) and Rathvon (2004) recommended that tests should have standard scores that go down to 69 or less and up to 131 or higher. The scores of tests that meet these criteria can be used to discriminate among individuals who are in the lower and higher levels of functioning. A look at the standard scores indicates that the TOSCRF forms have no ceiling effects at any age level. Floor effects are present only at the 7-year-old level. Because of this, the TOSCRF can be used to identify 7-year-old poor readers but not to determine their degree of reading difficulty. No floor effects were found for the other age groups (i.e., ages 8-0 to 18-11).

Descriptive Ratings for Standard Scores

Table 4.1

Standard Score	Description	% Included
>130	Very superior	2.34
121–130	Superior	6.87
111–120	Above average	16.12
90–110	Average	49.51
80–89	Below average	16.12
70–79	Poor	6.87
<70	Very poor	2.34

Percentile Ranks

Percentile ranks indicate the percentage of the distribution that is equal to or below a particular score. For example, a percentile rank of 56 means that 56% of the standardization sample scored at or below the student's score. Because this interpretation is easy to understand, percentile ranks are often used by practitioners when sharing test results with others. The distance between two percentile ranks increases as they move farther from the mean or average (i.e., the 50th percentile). Therefore, percentile ranks cannot be arithmetically manipulated (e.g., by adding, subtracting, or averaging the scores) in the same manner as standard scores. Raw scores are converted to percentile ranks using the *LANGUAGE! Online Assessment System.* Although percentile ranks are convenient and popular, examiners should be familiar with their advantages and disadvantages as explained by Aiken (2000), McLoughlin and Lewis (2001), and Salvia and Ysseldyke (2001).

Raw scores are converted to percentile ranks using the *LANGUAGE! Online Assessment System.* To obtain percentiles, raw scores along with the date on which the student was tested and birth date must be entered into the *LANGUAGE! Online Assessment System.*

Grade Equivalents

Grade equivalents for tests are usually labeled according to the content of the test. Thus, grade equivalents associated with tests of reading are called "reading grade levels."

Raw scores are converted to grade equivalents using the *LANGUAGE! Online Assessment System* or the conversion table.

For example, a Form A raw score of 80 yields a grade equivalent of 4.7. A grade equivalent of 4.7 indicates that the student's performance is similar to that of students in the normative sample who were in the 7th month of the 4th grade.

The TOSCRF reading grade equivalents were derived from the average scores of all examinees in the normative sample. The average raw score at four intervals for each grade were plotted on a graph, with raw scores on the vertical axis and grade on the horizontal axis. Lines were drawn connecting these average scores. After these lines had been smoothed and interpolated, the grade level that corresponded to each possible raw score was easily determined. For example, the average score on Form A that corresponded to students in fourth grade is 69 words identified correctly; any student obtaining a score of 69 receives a grade equivalent of 4.0.

Because interpolation, extrapolation, and smoothing are used to create grade equivalents, they should always be interpreted with caution. We provide them, reluctantly, only because some state and local policies require these types of scores. We urge TOSCRF users to read the concerns expressed by Aiken (2000), Anastasi and Urbina (1997), Linn and Miller (2005), and Salvia and Ysseldyke (2001) regarding the use of grade equivalents. The arguments against these scores focused on the fact that they are frequently misunderstood, have limited value statistically, require a good deal of subjective interpolation to calculate, and often give an unrealistic picture of a youngster's true abilities. We prefer that TOSCRF users employ standard scores or percentiles when possible.

Using Student Performance Results for Instructional Planning

The TOSCRF is primarily a measure of silent contextual reading fluency. Because TOSCRF scores reflect competence in so many aspects of reading (e.g., word identification, comprehension, fluency), they can be used to estimate general reading ability and to identify both good and poor readers.

Students who do well on the TOSCRF (i.e., whose standard scores are 90 or above) have profited greatly from early home and school experiences. Their parents and teachers probably have read to them often and provided them with an environment that is rich in opportunities to explore printed material. In school, these students perform normally or excel in reading and writing activities.

Students with low standard scores (i.e., below 90) on the TOSCRF will likely show deficiencies in all kinds of reading skills, including decoding, word identification, and comprehension skills. They are also very likely to be poor content readers. Because they are poor readers, they will likely have problems in written language skills, such as composition and spelling.

Performance in specific Steps within the *LANGUAGE!* curriculum is likely to have an impact on performance on the TOSCRF. Increased emphasis instructionally and more careful monitoring and analysis of performance on the Content Mastery tasks and Fluency tasks should be considered if TOSCRF performance is weak. For example:

Step	Description
Step 1: Phonemic Awareness and Phonics	Fluent sound-spelling correspondences can impact the speed of word recognition.
Step 2: Word Recognition and Spelling	Accurate and rapid word recognition as measured by Unit Word and Essential Word fluency drills in each unit can be tracked.
Step 3: Vocabulary and Morphology	Emphasis on learning the meaning of morphological markers contributes to improved understanding of grammar, which in turn facilitates understanding of the meaning of sentences.
Step 4: Grammar and Usage	Syntax is stressed through sentence expansion and sentence combining instruction and practice which can contribute to improved grammar knowledge.
Step 5: Listening and Speaking Comprehension	Provides for explicit development of phrasing techniques using the decodable reading selections. These techniques can help students to link knowledge of sentence structure to reading in meaningful phrases.

For further elaboration on the content of each Step in *LANGUAGE!*, turn to the *Teacher Resource Guide* for information on each Step of the instructional lesson.

Although the TOSCRF results may indicate that a particular student is reading at a level far below age expectancy, they do not indicate which reading skills are impaired or why the reading is below average. Poor readers need a thorough evaluation of their reading and reading-related abilities, which requires the use of additional tests, clinical instructional activities, structured interviews with parents and teachers, and reviews of case histories. Referrals to other professionals may be advisable.

Evaluating Growth Between Baseline and Progress Indicator

This section describes how to interpret growth for the TOSCRF. To evaluate whether a student has changed their relative standing in the national normative sample for the test, changes in standard scores (using the *Online Assessment System*) or grade equivalents must be examined.

Note: Because Baseline and Progress Indicators use alternate test forms (A and B), raw scores should not be compared across test forms.

Evaluating Growth Using Standard Scores

Standard scores show relative standing compared to others in the national normative sample for the test. A student must demonstrate a certain amount of growth in raw score to maintain his or her standard score (i.e., relative standing in the norming group).

To examine whether a student is improving her relative standing in the larger norming group for the test, examine the change in the student's standard score between the beginning of book (Baseline) and the end of book (Progress Indicator) assessment.

To understand how to evaluate growth using standard scores, note the following:

- An increase in a student's raw score does not necessarily mean an improvement in her standard score. For example, consider a student achieves a standard score on the Baseline test of 100, which represents the 50th percentile for any student age group. The student's raw score must improve relative to the norming sample at the student's age at the time of the Progress Indicator test in order to maintain a standard score of 100.
- When a student's standard score stays the same from Baseline to Progress Indicator, then she is maintaining her relative standing in the norming group. Students who maintain their relative standing (i.e., show no change in standard score) from year to year are showing an improvement in raw score performance.
- When a student's standard score increases from Baseline to Progress Indicator, then she is improving her relative standing in the norming group.
- When a student's standard score declines from Baseline to Progress Indicator, she is losing her relative standing in the norming group. This means that her raw score performance over the instructional period is either increasing (by an insufficient amount to register a standard score gain), staying the same, or declining.

Evaluating Growth Using Grade Equivalents

Grade equivalents represent the average score of students in the normative group for the test at each school grade.

To understand how to evaluate growth using grade equivalents, note the following:

- When a student's grade equivalent score increases between Baseline and Progress Indicator, the student is showing growth.

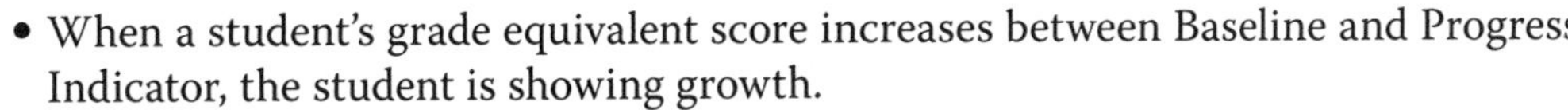

- The interpretation of an increase (or decrease) in grade equivalents depends on the size of increase.
- If the change in grade equivalent between Baseline and Progress Indicator is equal to the actual number of months in the school year that have passed, then the gain reflects a rate of growth that is expected based on average development.
- If the grade equivalent gain exceeds the number of months that have actually passed, then the gain reflects a rate of growth that is accelerated; that is, the gain exceeds a rate of growth that would be expected for average development.

TOSCRF Scoring Key

Baseline Form A

<table>
<tr><th></th><th></th><th>Line Word Count</th><th>Total Word Count</th></tr>
<tr><td>1.</td><td>YOU|CAN</td><td>2</td><td>2</td></tr>
<tr><td>2.</td><td>LOOK|DOWN</td><td>2</td><td>4</td></tr>
<tr><td>3.</td><td>JUMP|UP|RUN|FAST</td><td>4</td><td>8</td></tr>
<tr><td>4.</td><td>SEE|FATHER|WE|SING</td><td>4</td><td>12</td></tr>
<tr><td>5.</td><td>A|YELLOW|BIRD|WITH|BLUE|WINGS|SAT|ON|MOTHERS|PRETTY
HAT|IT|WAS|THE|MISSING|BIRD</td><td>10
6</td><td>22
28</td></tr>
<tr><td>6.</td><td>THE|FOX|GAVE|THE|STORK|A|BIT|OF|THE|SOUP|IN|A|SHALLOW
DISH|BUT|THE|STORK|COULD|NOT|EAT|FROM|THE|DISH</td><td>13
10</td><td>41
51</td></tr>
<tr><td>7.</td><td>THE|BOYS|WENT|INTO|A|STORE|AND|LOOKED|AT|BOOKS|ABOUT
ANIMALS|ONE|BOY|SAW|A|BOOK|ABOUT|HORSES</td><td>11
8</td><td>62
70</td></tr>
<tr><td>8.</td><td>THE|STORK|SERVED|THE|SOUP|IN|TWO|TALL|BOTTLES|WITH
THIN|NARROW|NECKS|SHE|STUCK|HER|LONG|BILL|INTO|THE
BOTTLE|AND|ATE|EVERY|DROP</td><td>10
10
5</td><td>80
90
95</td></tr>
<tr><td>9.</td><td>SOME|DAYS|AFTERWARD|THE|STORK|INVITED|THE|FOX|TO
DINNER|SHE|HAD|MADE|SOME|DELICIOUS|SOUP|AND|THE|FOX
WAS|VERY|HUNGRY</td><td>9
10
3</td><td>104
114
117</td></tr>
<tr><td>10.</td><td>AS|THE|CLOCK|TICKED|OFF|ONE|MINUTE|AFTER|ANOTHER
EACH|OF|THE|GIRLS|TRIED|TO|PIN|A|RIBBON|ON|THE|LIONS
TAIL|THEY|PUT|RIBBONS|ON|THE|LIONS|PAWS|HEAD|AND
BODY|WHICH|GAVE|HIM|A|FRIENDLY|LOOK</td><td>9
12
10
7</td><td>126
138
148
155</td></tr>
<tr><td>11.</td><td>THIS|MAN|WAS|ONE|OF|THE|FIRST|EUROPEAN|TRAVELERS|TO
VISIT|THE|DISTANT|REGION|OF|CHINA|HE|LEARNED|SEVERAL
LANGUAGES|SPOKEN|THERE|AND|SERVED|ITS|GREAT|RULERS
FOR|MANY|YEARS</td><td>10
9
8
3</td><td>165
174
182
185</td></tr>
</table>

<table>
<tr><th></th><th></th><th>Line Word Count</th><th>Total Word Count</th></tr>
<tr><td>12.</td><td>AS|A|YOUTH|HE|TRAVELED|FROM|ONE|FARM|TO|ANOTHER</td><td>10</td><td>195</td></tr>
<tr><td></td><td>PICKING|CROPS|AS|THEY|RIPENED|SINCE|HIS|FAMILY|HAD</td><td>9</td><td>204</td></tr>
<tr><td></td><td>NO|PERMANENT|HOME|HE|HAD|ATTENDED|A|MULTITUDE</td><td>8</td><td>212</td></tr>
<tr><td></td><td>OF|DIFFERENT|SCHOOLS|BY|THE|TIME|HE|REACHED</td><td>8</td><td>220</td></tr>
<tr><td></td><td>THE|SEVENTH|GRADE</td><td>3</td><td>223</td></tr>
<tr><td>13.</td><td>THE|YOUNG|MAN|WAS|DELIGHTED|TO|OBTAIN|HIS|DEPUTY</td><td>9</td><td>232</td></tr>
<tr><td></td><td>SHERIFFS|BADGE|AS|HIS|FIRST|ASSIGNMENT|HE|HAD|BEEN</td><td>9</td><td>241</td></tr>
<tr><td></td><td>APPOINTED|TO|ESCORT|A|PRISONER|TO|THE|AUTHORITIES|AT</td><td>9</td><td>250</td></tr>
<tr><td></td><td>THE|COUNTY|SEAT|AND|THE|SITE|OF|THE|IMPENDING|TRIAL</td><td>10</td><td>260</td></tr>
<tr><td>14.</td><td>THERE|ARE|SUNDRY|DEFINITIONS|OF|JAZZ|ALL|OF|THEM|VAGUE</td><td>10</td><td>270</td></tr>
<tr><td></td><td>THEIR|VAGUENESS|SEEMS|IMPERATIVE|HOWEVER|IF|THEY</td><td>7</td><td>277</td></tr>
<tr><td></td><td>ARE|TO|ACCOMMODATE|THE|CUSTOM|OF|JAZZ|TO|APPROPRIATE</td><td>9</td><td>286</td></tr>
<tr><td></td><td>EVERYTHING|IN|SIGHT</td><td>3</td><td>289</td></tr>
<tr><td>15.</td><td>AS|THE|EMPERORS|AGENT|HE|EXPLORED|THE|FAR|CORNERS</td><td>9</td><td>298</td></tr>
<tr><td></td><td>OF|THE|KINGDOM|HE|KEPT|A|NOTEBOOK|FILLED|WITH</td><td>9</td><td>307</td></tr>
<tr><td></td><td>FASCINATING|ACCOUNTS|OF|HIS|EXPERIENCES|AS|WELL|AS</td><td>8</td><td>315</td></tr>
<tr><td></td><td>ECONOMIC|AND|POLITICAL|REPORTS|FOR|THE|EMPERORS|USE</td><td>8</td><td>323</td></tr>
<tr><td>16.</td><td>THE|ADROIT|MAN|WAS|AFFABLE|IN|DEBATE|AND|OF|THAT</td><td>10</td><td>333</td></tr>
<tr><td></td><td>SEEMING|HUMILITY|AND|SUBMISSION|OF|JUDGMENT|AS|IF|HE</td><td>9</td><td>342</td></tr>
<tr><td></td><td>BROUGHT|NO|OPINIONS|WITH|HIM|BUT|RATHER|A|FIDELITY|TO</td><td>10</td><td>352</td></tr>
<tr><td></td><td>ENLIGHTENMENT|AND|INSTRUCTION|HE|HAD|SO|SUBTLE</td><td>7</td><td>359</td></tr>
<tr><td></td><td>A|WAY|OF|INTERROGATING|THE|OTHER|MINISTERS|AND|UNDER</td><td>9</td><td>368</td></tr>
<tr><td></td><td>THE|GUISE|OF|SKEPTICISM|INSINUATING|HIS|OBJECTIONS</td><td>7</td><td>375</td></tr>
<tr><td></td><td>TO|A|PROPOSED|EDICT|THAT|HE|INSTILLED|HIS|PERSPECTIVE</td><td>9</td><td>384</td></tr>
<tr><td></td><td>IN|THOSE|FROM|WHOM|HE|PRETENDED|TO|LEARN</td><td>8</td><td>392</td></tr>
<tr><td>17.</td><td>CERTAINLY|SHE|HAD|LATELY|BEEN|COGNIZANT|OF|THE|SUAVE</td><td>9</td><td>401</td></tr>
<tr><td></td><td>YOUNG|MANS|UNNECESSARY|CHIVALRY|BUT|SHE|HAD</td><td>7</td><td>408</td></tr>
<tr><td></td><td>CONSTRUED|IT|WAS|AN|ABERRATION|OF|JUDGMENT|OR|TASTE</td><td>9</td><td>417</td></tr>
<tr><td></td><td>AS|ONE|PROOF|AMONG|OTHERS|THAT|HE|HAD|NOT|ALWAYS</td><td>10</td><td>427</td></tr>
<tr><td></td><td>MOVED|IN|THE|BEST|CIRCLES|THAT|WITH|ALL|HIS|ASSIDUOUS</td><td>10</td><td>437</td></tr>
<tr><td></td><td>CONCERN|FOR|HER|THE|ACCOUTREMENTS|OF|TRUE</td><td>7</td><td>444</td></tr>
<tr><td></td><td>GENTILITY|WERE|WANTING|BUT|UNTIL|NOW|SHE|HAD|NEVER</td><td>9</td><td>453</td></tr>
<tr><td></td><td>SURMISED|IT|TO|MEAN|ANYTHING|HIS|MANNER|MUST|HAVE</td><td>9</td><td>462</td></tr>
<tr><td></td><td>BEEN|EQUIVOCAL|OR|SHE|COULD|NOT|HAVE|BEEN|SO|BEGUILED</td><td>10</td><td>472</td></tr>
</table>

TOSCRF Scoring Key

Progress Indicator Form B

<table>
<tr><th></th><th></th><th>Line Word Count</th><th>Total Word Count</th></tr>
<tr><td>1.</td><td>GO|HOME</td><td>2</td><td>2</td></tr>
<tr><td>2.</td><td>STOP|NOW</td><td>2</td><td>4</td></tr>
<tr><td>3.</td><td>HELP|ME|RIDE|FAST</td><td>4</td><td>8</td></tr>
<tr><td>4.</td><td>SIT|DOWN|LOOK|AROUND</td><td>4</td><td>12</td></tr>
<tr><td>5.</td><td>TWO|GIRLS|WENT|TO|A|FARM|FOR|A|VISIT|THERE|WERE|COWS
PIGS|DUCKS|AND|FIVE|HENS|THE|GIRLS|GATHERED|THE
EGGS|EVERY|MORNING</td><td>12
9
3</td><td>24
33
36</td></tr>
<tr><td>6.</td><td>FATHER|WENT|OUT|TO|BUY|SOME|PRETTY|FLOWERS|THE|CAKE
COOKED|A|LITTLE|TOO|LONG|SO|IT|WAS|BROWN</td><td>10
9</td><td>46
55</td></tr>
<tr><td>7.</td><td>JUST|AS|THE|CHILDREN|WERE|READY|TO|RUN|THE|RAIN|BEGAN
TO|FALL|THE|TEACHER|SAID|HURRY|IN|CHILDREN</td><td>11
8</td><td>66
74</td></tr>
<tr><td>8.</td><td>ONCE|THERE|WAS|A|TURTLE|WHO|CHATTERED|SO|MUCH|THAT
SHE|HAD|NO|FRIENDS|ONE|DAY|SHE|MET|AN|EAGLE|TRAVELING
TO|DISTANT|LANDS|ACROSS|THE|SEA</td><td>10
11
6</td><td>84
95
101</td></tr>
<tr><td>9.</td><td>ONE|BRIGHT|SUMMER|DAY|A|YOUNG|BOY|AND|HIS|GRANDMOTHER
WALKED|TO|A|NEARBY|POND|TO|FISH|THE|BOYS|GRANDMOTHER
SHOWED|HIM|HOW|TO|PUT|WORMS|ON|THE|HOOKS|SO|THEY|WOULD
NOT|COME|OFF</td><td>10
10
12
3</td><td>111
121
133
136</td></tr>
<tr><td>10.</td><td>FARMERS|ATTEMPT|TO|CONTROL|PESTS|BY|USING|CHEMICALS
BUT|THEY|CAN|MAKE|OUR|FOOD|UNSAFE|TO|EAT|AT|ANY|SEASON
OF|THE|YEAR|WEATHER|MAY|ALSO|DESTROY|CROPS</td><td>8
12
8</td><td>144
156
164</td></tr>
<tr><td>11.</td><td>DURING|THE|FILMING|OF|A|MOVIE|STARS|HAVE|AN|EXHAUSTING
SCHEDULE|THEIR|DAY|OFTEN|BEGINS|BEFORE|DAWN|WITH
MAKEUP|SESSIONS|COSTUME|FITTINGS|OR|SPECIAL|TRAINING
WITH|A|SPEECH|COACH</td><td>10
8
7
4</td><td>174
182
189
193</td></tr>
</table>

<table>
<tr><th></th><th></th><th>Line Word Count</th><th>Total Word Count</th></tr>
<tr><td>12.</td><td>ALL|OVER|THE|WORLD|FARMERS|FACE|DIFFICULT|PROBLEMS</td><td>8</td><td>201</td></tr>
<tr><td></td><td>FRUIT|VEGETABLES|AND|OTHER|PLANTS|ARE|FREQUENTLY</td><td>7</td><td>208</td></tr>
<tr><td></td><td>ATTACKED|BY|HARMFUL|INSECTS|AND|DISEASES|THAT|CAN</td><td>8</td><td>216</td></tr>
<tr><td></td><td>WIPE|OUT|AN|ENTIRE|CROP</td><td>5</td><td>221</td></tr>
<tr><td>13.</td><td>THE|PARK|RANGERS|SOLITARY|VIGIL|WAS|TERMINATED|BY</td><td>8</td><td>229</td></tr>
<tr><td></td><td>THE|STIR|OF|HOOVES|IN|THE|SCRUB|THROUGH|THE|EARLY</td><td>10</td><td>239</td></tr>
<tr><td></td><td>DIMNESS|SHE|COULD|PERCEIVE|THE|FLUID|CONTOURS|OF</td><td>8</td><td>247</td></tr>
<tr><td></td><td>THE|MAJESTIC|CREATURES|AS|THEY|ASSEMBLED|AT</td><td>7</td><td>254</td></tr>
<tr><td></td><td>THE|ARTESIAN|SPRING</td><td>3</td><td>257</td></tr>
<tr><td>14.</td><td>THE|GALES|FURY|BEGAN|TO|INTENSIFY|AS|THE|STEADFAST</td><td>9</td><td>266</td></tr>
<tr><td></td><td>GIRL|LUGGED|THE|SPLINTERED|ROWBOAT|ONTO|THE|BARREN</td><td>8</td><td>274</td></tr>
<tr><td></td><td>REEF|HER|YOUNGER|BROTHER|HAD|MANAGED|TO|STUMBLE</td><td>8</td><td>282</td></tr>
<tr><td></td><td>TO|SHORE|THROUGH|THE|CHURNING|SURF|DESPITE|THE|GASH</td><td>9</td><td>291</td></tr>
<tr><td></td><td>ON|HIS|LEG|AND|POSSIBLY|A|FRACTURED|WRIST</td><td>8</td><td>299</td></tr>
<tr><td>15.</td><td>THIS|FAMOUS|AMERICAN|WOMAN|BECAME|THE|LEADER|OF</td><td>8</td><td>307</td></tr>
<tr><td></td><td>THE|UNDERGROUND|RAILROAD|A|SECRET|NETWORK|OF</td><td>7</td><td>317</td></tr>
<tr><td></td><td>HOUSEHOLDS|THAT|PROVIDED|FOOD|AND|SHELTER|TO</td><td>7</td><td>321</td></tr>
<tr><td></td><td>RUNAWAY|SLAVES|SHE|LED|GROUPS|OF|SLAVES|FROM|ONE</td><td>9</td><td>330</td></tr>
<tr><td></td><td>POINT|TO|ANOTHER|ON|THE|PERILOUS|JOURNEY|NORTH</td><td>8</td><td>338</td></tr>
<tr><td>16.</td><td>A|LEGEND|IS|A|TRADITIONAL|ORAL|NARRATIVE|REGARDED</td><td>8</td><td>346</td></tr>
<tr><td></td><td>AS|TRUE|BY|ITS|TELLER|AND|THE|SOCIETY|IN|WHICH|IT</td><td>11</td><td>357</td></tr>
<tr><td></td><td>CIRCULATES|LIKE|OTHER|CATEGORIES|OF|FOLKLORE</td><td>6</td><td>363</td></tr>
<tr><td></td><td>LEGENDS|FREQUENTLY|BECOME|EMBELLISHED|WITH</td><td>5</td><td>368</td></tr>
<tr><td></td><td>EXAGGERATED|OR|SUPERNATURAL|ELEMENTS|THAT|MAKE</td><td>6</td><td>374</td></tr>
<tr><td></td><td>THEM|HIGHLY|IMPLAUSIBLE</td><td>3</td><td>377</td></tr>
<tr><td>17.</td><td>THE|QUEEN|WAS|ONE|OF|THE|POTENTATES|WHO|ATTEMPTED</td><td>9</td><td>386</td></tr>
<tr><td></td><td>THINGS|THAT|NO|REPUTABLE|SOVEREIGN|WOULD|HAVE</td><td>7</td><td>393</td></tr>
<tr><td></td><td>DARED|VENTURE|ON|AND|ACHIEVED|THOSE|IN|WHICH|NONE</td><td>9</td><td>402</td></tr>
<tr><td></td><td>BUT|THE|MOST|INTREPID|COULD|HAVE|SUCCEEDED|SHE</td><td>8</td><td>410</td></tr>
<tr><td></td><td>CONSULTED|WITH|VERY|FEW|UPON|ANY|ACTION|OF|IMPORT</td><td>9</td><td>419</td></tr>
<tr><td></td><td>NOR|CONVEYED|ANY|ENTERPRISE|WITH|MORE|THAN|THOSE</td><td>8</td><td>427</td></tr>
<tr><td></td><td>WHO|WERE|TO|HAVE|PRINCIPAL|PARTS|IN|THE|EXECUTION</td><td>9</td><td>436</td></tr>
<tr><td></td><td>OF|IT|NO|SOONER|THAN|WAS|ABSOLUTELY|NECESSARY</td><td>8</td><td>444</td></tr>
</table>

Converting Raw Scores to Grade Equivalents for Book A

Converting TOSCRF Baseline Form A and Progress Indicator Form B Raw Scores to Grade Equivalents			
Grade Equivalent	Baseline Form A	Progress Indicator Form B	Grade Equivalent
1.0	25–28	25–28	1.0
1.2	29–31	29–32	1.2
1.4	32–35	33–36	1.4
1.7	36–40	37–40	1.7
2.0	41–43	41–44	2.0
2.2	44–47	45–47	2.2
2.4	48–50	48–51	2.4
2.7	51–53	52–54	2.7
3.0	54–58	55–58	3.0
3.2	59–61	59–62	3.2
3.4	62–65	63–65	3.4
3.7	66–68	66–69	3.7
4.0	69–72	70–73	4.0
4.2	73–75	74–76	4.2
4.4	76–79	77–79	4.4
4.7	80–82	80–82	4.7
5.0	83–84	83–84	5.0
5.2	85–86	85–87	5.2
5.4	87–88	88–90	5.4
5.7	89–93	91–93	5.7
6.0	94–96	94–96	6.0
6.2	97–99	97–99	6.2
6.4	100–101	100–102	6.4
6.7	102–104	103–104	6.7
7.0	105–107	105–107	7.0
7.2	108–110	108–109	7.2

Grade Equivalent	Baseline Form A	Progress Indicator Form B	Grade Equivalent
7.4	111–112	110–111	7.4
7.7	113–114	112–114	7.7
8.0	115–117	115–117	8.0
8.2	118–119	118–119	8.2
8.4	120–122	120–121	8.4
8.7	123–124	122–123	8.7
9.0	125–126	124–125	9.0
9.2	127–128	126–127	9.2
9.4	129–130	128–129	9.4
9.7	131–132	130–131	9.7
10.0	133–134	132–133	10.0
10.2	135–136	134–135	10.2
10.4	137–138	136	10.4
10.7	139	137–138	10.7
11.0	140–141	139–140	11.0
11.2	142–143	141–142	11.2
11.4	144–145	143	11.4
11.7	146	144–145	11.7
12.0	147	146	12.0
12.2	148–149	147	12.2
12.4	150	148	12.4
12.7	151–152	149–150	12.7
13.0	>152	>150	13.0

LANGUAGE! Reading Scale (LRS)

Description

The *LANGUAGE!* Reading Scale (LRS) was developed using the Lexile Framework® for Reading. The Lexile Framework for Reading is a normed measurement system that measures reading comprehension. This means that The *LANGUAGE!* Reading Scale test results can be linked to the Lexile national norms to measure how well readers comprehend expository text.

The LRS test has the following features:

- Consists of seven nonfiction passages on a variety of topics; the passages are arranged in order of increasing text difficulty.
- Test items are formed by the deletion of words from the passages. For each missing word, four possible words are provided. Students are asked to select the best word to fill in the blank.
- When considered in the context of the sentence with the word deletion, each word choice is plausible, both semantically and syntactically. When the missing word is considered within the context of the surrounding text, however, only one response is correct. Thus, responding correctly requires understanding (i.e., comprehending) the text surrounding the word. The words do not draw on background knowledge but depend on information in the passage; all information needed to answer correctly is provided in the passage.
- Yields a raw score and percentile rank. The test also reports a Lexile measure that represents a students' current reading ability in terms of the most difficult text in Lexile measures that the students can comprehend with assistance from teachers or parents.
- Is group-administered, untimed and can be completed within one 50-minute class period.

The student's results are reported as a Lexile measure. The Lexile Framework® for Reading provides teachers and educators with tools to help them link assessment results with subsequent instruction. Assessments such as those in *LANGUAGE!* that are linked to the Lexile scale provide tools for monitoring the progress of students at any time during the course. Readers interested in additional information about the Lexile Framework® for Reading and its correlation to many other well-established tests of reading comprehension should see the *LANGUAGE! Reading Scale Technical Guide* found at www. teachlanguage.com.

Administration and Scoring Procedures

This section explains how to administer and score the LRS. The discussion includes (a) basic testing procedures, and (b) specific instructions for administering and scoring the LRS.

Basic Testing Procedures

The chart below shows which forms should be used for the LRS Baseline and Progress Indicator tests.

	Baseline	Progress Indicator
Test Form	Student *Baseline and Summative Assessment* booklet, Form A, page 9	Student *Baseline and Summative Assessment* booklet, Form B, page 41
When to administer	Before Unit 1	Unit 6

Providing practice with standardized test-taking procedures

One way to provide students an opportunity to practice standardized test-taking procedures is to have them record their answers onto a student answer form. A corresponding scoring key can be found on page 88 for Baseline, Form A and Progress Indicator, Form B. If you want to use the Student Answer Form, distribute one to each student and ask them to write their names and the date on the form before reading the directions.

The examiner can assure a reliable administration of the test by adhering to the following simple rules:

1. Review these directions for administering the LRS tests prior to the testing session.
2. In order to ensure a uniform administration across all students who take these tests, it is very important that you read aloud **WORD FOR WORD** the bolded text that follows the word "SAY." The material in italic is information for you and should not be read to the students.
3. Repeat the directions as many times as needed.
4. Allow about 50 minutes for students to complete the test. Each test administration should take place in one class period.

This test can be administered to entire classes, to small groups, or to individual students (e.g., to a student receiving remedial instruction or to a special education student). The same instructions are used for all forms.

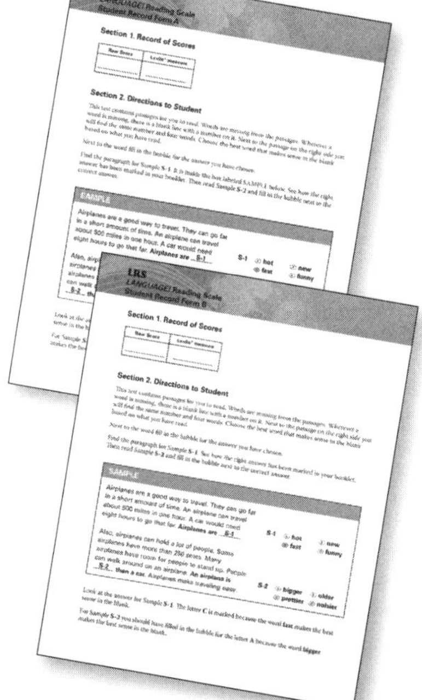
LRS
LANGUAGE! Reading Scale
Student Record Form A
Section 1. Record of Scores
Section 2. Directions to Student
SAMPLE

LRS
LANGUAGE! Reading Scale
Student Record Form B
Section 1. Record of Scores
Section 2. Directions to Student
SAMPLE

Specific Administration Instructions

The following administration instructions apply to the LRS test when given either as a Baseline (Form A) or as a Progress Indicator (Form B) test.

To administer the LRS, each student will need two sharpened No. 2 pencils.

<u>Step 1:</u>

Distribute students' Baseline and Summative Assessment *booklets. Have students turn to page 9 for Baseline or page 41 for Progress Indicator assessment in their booklets. Check to see that students are on the correct page.*

Step 2:

SAY:

- **Do not turn the page until I tell you to.**

Once all students have opened to the correct page, continue below.

SAY:

- **Find where it says "Directions to the Student"** *(point)*. **Read silently while I read out loud.**

Hold up a test booklet to show the students the correct page. Check that all students have opened their booklets to the correct page. When everyone has found the page:

SAY:

- **Today you will take the *LANGUAGE!* Reading Scale test. This reading test contains passages for you to read. Words are missing from the passages. Where a word is missing, there is a blank line with a number on it. Next to the passage on the right side, you will find the same number and four words. These are the answer choices. Read each sentence carefully, and then choose the best word to complete the sentence based on what you have read. Next to the word you will fill in the bubble for the answer you have chosen.**

SAY:

- **Find the paragraph for Sample S-1. It is inside the box labeled SAMPLE.**

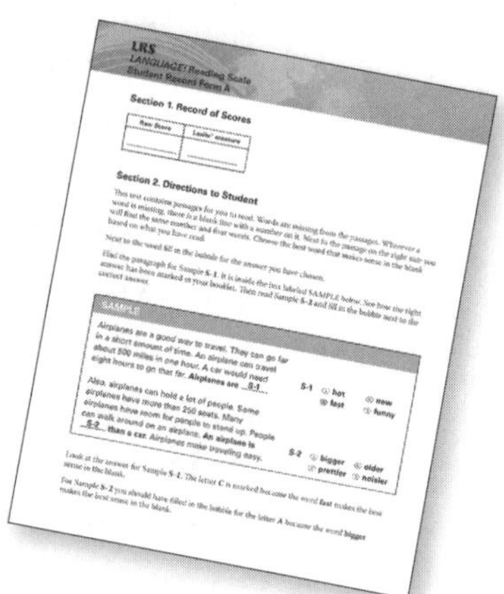
LRS
LANGUAGE! Reading Scale
Student Record Form A

Section 1. Record of Scores

Section 2. Directions to Student

SAMPLE

Teachers should not read the sample items out loud. They are printed here only for the teacher's information.

Next, hold up the test booklet to point to the paragraph for Sample S-1. When everyone has found the paragraph,

SAY:

- **Read the paragraph for Sample S-1.**

If students are using a separate answer form, then hold up an answer sheet and point to the words "SAMPLE ITEMS." When everyone has found the section:

SAY:

- **On your answer sheet, find the answer for Sample S-1. The bubble for the letter 'C' is filled in because the word "fast" makes the best sense in the blank.**

  Now do Sample S-2 on your own.

Give students time to complete Sample S-2 by themselves. Then proceed to Step 3 below.

If students are using the test booklet:

SAY:

- **Look at the answer for Sample S-1. The bubble for the letter 'C' is filled in because the word "fast" makes the best sense in the blank.**

  Now do Sample S-2 on your own.

Give students time to complete Sample S-2 by themselves. Then proceed to Step 3 below.

If students are using a separate answer form:

Step 3:

SAY:

- **On your answer sheet, find the same number as the blank. Fill in the bubble next to the answer you have chosen for Sample S-2. Remember to completely fill in the circle corresponding to the answer you choose.**

If students are using the test booklet:

Step 3:

SAY:

- **Fill in the bubble next to the answer you have chosen for Sample S-2. Remember to completely fill in the circle corresponding to the answer you choose.**

Step 4:

After students have completed Sample S-2:

SAY:

- **For Sample S-2 you should have filled in the bubble for the letter "A" because the word "bigger" makes the best sense in the blank.**

Assist students who do not understand the instructions. When everyone is ready:

SAY:

- **Now turn your test booklet to the next page. Look at the rest of the directions. Read them silently while I them out loud. Before you begin working in your test booklet, here are a few reminders:**
  - Do your best to read as many of the passages as you can and to complete as many of the items as you can.
  - There is no time limit, so work carefully and do not rush.
  - Be sure to choose the best answer based on the information in the passage.
  - Remember to mark only one answer choice for each item.
  - If you want to change your answer, be sure to erase or cross out your first mark. Then mark the answer you want.
  - Check all of your answers after completing the test.
  - You may not be sure of the answer until you have read the sentences that come after the blank. Be sure to read enough to choose your answer.

If students are using a separate answer form, hold up a Student Answer Form and point to Question 1. When everyone has found Question 1 on their answer sheet:

SAY:

- **This is where you will mark your answer to Question 1. Now turn your test booklet to Question 1. You may now begin working in your booklet.**

If students are using the test booklet, hold up the test booklet and point to Question 1. When everyone has found Question 1 in their test booklet:

SAY:

- **Now turn your test booklet to Question 1. This is where you will mark your answer to Question 1. You may now begin working in your booklet.**

After students have begun the test:

- *Check to make sure that each student is following the directions.*
- *You may help individual students, as long as assistance is limited to mechanical aspects of marking answers and clarifying directions. DO NOT do the following:*
  - *Indicate a correct answer.*
  - *Tell students words in the passage.*
  - *Provide clues for answering an item.*
- *If a student is marking answers without reading test items, encourage the student to study each item carefully.*

After students have done all they can:

- *Tell students to stop and collect all student answer forms and student* Baseline and Summative Assessment *booklets.*

Scoring the LRS Tests

Score the test using the answer keys for Baseline Form A and Progress Indicator Form B on page 88 of this booklet.

The raw score is the total number of items answered correctly.

Interpreting the LRS Results

This section presents information about interpreting the LRS results.

The topics to be addressed include (a) how to record the scores, (b) how to interpret the scores, (c) using student performance for instructional planning, and (d) how to evaluate growth between Baseline and Progress Indicator.

Recording of LRS Scores

Converting raw scores to Lexile® measures can happen in two ways: manually or by using the *Online Assessment System*. The *Online Assessment System* provides users with the scores listed in the table below. Without use of the *Online Assessment System* (manual recording of scores), only Lexiles are provided.

Scores Provided	
Online Assessment System	Manual
Converts raw scores to: • Lexile® measures • percentile ranks **Note:** no need to use print record forms	Converts raw scores to: • Lexile® measure **Note:** must use print record forms: LRS Student Record Form, Summary Record Form, Baseline and Progress Indicator Class Roster.

Recording Using the *LANGUAGE! Online Assessment System*

Enter raw scores into the *LANGUAGE! Online Assessment System*. The Web-based data entry and reporting system will convert raw scores to Lexile measures and percentile ranks.

Detailed discussions of the Lexile scores and percentile ranks are found in the "Test Scores and Their Interpretation" section of this chapter.

Manual Recording

Use the conversion table to convert the LRS raw scores to Lexile measures. For example: A raw score of 38 on Form A converts to a Lexile measure of 410 (410L). A detailed discussion of Lexile measures is found in the next section.

Once Lexiles are obtained, scores should be recorded on the print record forms:

- **Lexile Student Record Form**—An individual's test performance is recorded on the LRS Student Record Form in the student *Baseline and Summative Assessment* on page 9 for Baseline Form A and page 41 for Progress Indicator Form B.
- **Summary Record Form**—This form summarizes all Baseline and Summative Assessment scores for an individual. This form can be found in the student *Baseline and Summative Assessment*, on page 61.
- **Baseline and Progress Indicator Class Roster**—This form summarizes all Baseline and Progress Indicator assessment scores (not including writing) for a class. Transfer scores from the students' Summary Record Forms to the Baseline and Progress Indicator Class Roster found in Appendix B.

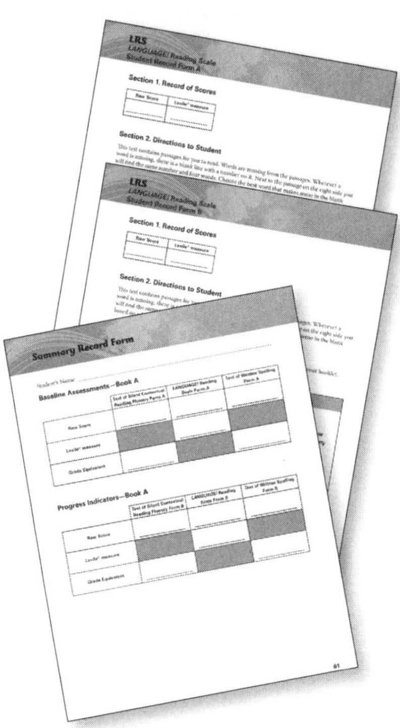

Test Scores and Their Interpretation

The chart below shows the scores provided for the LRS: raw scores, Lexile measures, and percentile ranks. This section includes a brief discussion of each score and how it should be interpreted. The shortcomings of these scores and cautions about their use are also discussed.

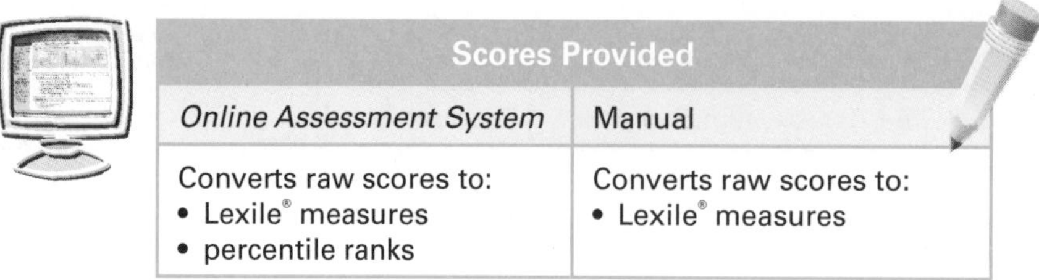

Scores Provided	
Online Assessment System	Manual
Converts raw scores to: • Lexile® measures • percentile ranks	Converts raw scores to: • Lexile® measures

Raw Scores

A student's raw score on the test is the number of items the student answered correctly. For example, if a student correctly answered 16 items on the 49-item test, his or her raw score would be 16. Because each form of the *LANGUAGE! Reading Scale* has a different difficulty level, raw scores on different forms should not be compared. To compare results for different forms, the raw score should first be converted to a Lexile measure.

Lexile Measures

A **Lexile® reader measure** represents a student's reading ability on the Lexile scale. The Lexile scale is a scale for reporting reading ability, so a higher number represents a higher level of reading ability. A Lexile reader measure is reported in intervals of 5L (Lexile), from a low of 5L to a high of 2000L. Readers who score at or below a reported level of 5L receive a score of BR (Beginning Reader). A student's score on the *LANGUAGE! Reading Scale* is reported as a Lexile reader measure.

> Raw scores are converted to Lexile reader measures using the *LANGUAGE! Online Assessment System* or the conversion table.

A **Lexile® text measure** represents a text's difficulty level on the Lexile scale. A Lexile text measure, like a Lexile reader measure, is reported on the Lexile scale. A Lexile text measure is reported in intervals of 10L, from a low of 10L to a high of 2000L. The lower a book's Lexile measure, the easier it will likely be to comprehend. For example, a text with a Lexile measure of 850L will most likely be easier for a reader to comprehend than a text at 950L. A Lexile text measure of 10L or below is reported as BR, which means that the text is appropriate for a Beginning Reader. The text selections within *LANGUAGE!* have been rated on the Lexile text measure scale.

The **Lexile reader measure** and the **Lexile text measure** can be used together to predict how well a student will likely comprehend a text at a specific Lexile level. For example, if a student has a Lexile measure of 1000L, she will be forecasted to comprehend approximately 75 percent of a book with the same Lexile measure (1000L). When the Lexile measure and the Lexile scale were developed, the 75-percent comprehension rate was set as the point where the difference between the Lexile reader measure and the Lexile text measure is 0L. The 75-percent comprehension rate is called "targeted" reading. This rate is based on independent reading; if the student receives assistance, the comprehension rate will increase. The target reading rate is the point at which a student will comprehend enough to understand the text, but will also face some reading challenge. At this challenge point, a reader is not bored by text that is too easy, but also does not experience too much difficulty in understanding.

When a reader takes the LRS Baseline or Progress Indicator test, his or her results are reported as a Lexile® measure. This means, for example, that a student whose reading ability has been measured at 500L is expected to read with 75-percent comprehension a book that is also measured at 500L. When the reader and text are matched (same Lexile measures), the reader is "targeted." A targeted reader reports confidence, competence, and control over the text. When a text measure is 250L above the reader's measure, comprehension is predicted to drop to 50 percent and the reader will likely experience frustration and inadequacy. Conversely, when a text measure is 250L below the reader's measure, comprehension is predicted to go up to 90% and the reader is expected to experience control and fluency. When reading a book within his or her Lexile range (50L above his or her Lexile measure to 100L below), the reader is forecasted to comprehend enough of the text to make sense of it, while still being challenged enough to maintain interest and learning.

Percentile Ranks

Percentile ranks indicate the percentage of the distribution that is equal to or below a particular score. For example, a percentile rank of 80 means that 80% of the norming sample scored at or below the student's score, and 20% of the norming sample scored above the student's score. The norming sample for the Lexile Framework for Reading included a nationally-representative sample of students. Because this interpretation is easy to understand, percentile ranks are often used by practitioners when sharing test results with others. The distance between two percentile ranks increases as they move farther from the mean or average (i.e., the 50th percentile). Therefore, percentile ranks cannot be arithmetically manipulated (e.g., by adding, subtracting, or averaging the scores) in the same manner as standard scores. Raw scores are converted to percentile ranks using the *LANGUAGE! Online Assessment System*. Although percentile ranks are convenient and popular, examiners should be familiar with their advantages and disadvantages as explained by Aiken (2000), McLoughlin and Lewis (2001), and Salvia and Ysseldyke (2001).

Raw scores are converted to percentile ranks using the *LANGUAGE! Online Assessment System*.

Using Student Performance for Instructional Planning

The *LANGUAGE! Reading Scale* tests are designed to measure reading comprehension and facilitate student growth by appropriately targeting instructional materials to a student's reading ability. The LRS assessment results indicate how much information the student understands while reading. The level of understanding is expressed in terms of a Lexile measure. Using the Lexile measure to match a student to reading material helps reduce frustration or boredom.

Baseline Assessment and Progress Indicators

Within *LANGUAGE!*: All three levels of text selections (Decodable/Independent, Instructional, and Challenge) in *LANGUAGE!* have been rated and assigned a Lexile® text measure. This information allows teachers to make decisions about the text selections within the curriculum that students can read independently and text for which they will need instructional support. The Lexile range for a reader is 50L above his or her Lexile measure to 100L below. For example, a reader with a Lexile meaure of 350L would have a Lexile range of 250–400L. If the Lexile text measure for a selection is within the student's Lexile range, the student should be able to read and comprehend that text with 75% comprehension. When the text selection is too difficult for the students to read, teachers can use another options, such as reading to the students or reading chorally.

In addition to the value of a text-to-reader match facilitated by LRS, sluggish gains in Lexile points on the Progress Indicators can indicate the need for instructional focus in all of the Steps in *LANGUAGE!*. The following table identifies the potential contribution from each Step to strengthen reading comprehension and allow for improved performance on this test.

Step	Why focus
Step 1: Phonemic Awareness and Phonics	Accurate and automatic sound-spelling correspondences contribute to accurate word recognition.
Step 2: Word Recognition and Spelling	Accurate and automatic recognition of words frees up attention to the more complex tasks involved in reading. Use of syllable and meaning parts in longer words helps decode multisyllabic words which often carry the new concept load of reading material, particularly in content area (expository) text.
Step 3: Vocabulary and Morphology	Knowledge of multiple meanings, context-based vocabulary strategies, and meaning parts contribute to comprehension of text.
Step 4: Grammar and Usage	Knowledge of grammatical and syntactical structures allows students to decipher increasingly complex and syntactically embedded sentences often found in content area text.
Step 5: Listening and Reading Comprehension	Opportunities to listen to more complex text build background knowledge and vocabulary which contribute to greater text comprehension.
Step 6: Speaking and Writing	Writing reinforces understanding of text structure. Writing often requires understanding of text material to select and organize information in preparation to write a paragraph, essay or report.

For further elaboration on the content of each Step in *LANGUAGE!*, turn to the *Teacher Resource Guide* for information on each step of the instructional lesson.

Outside the curriculum materials: Teachers can also use the Lexile measure attained by students to help them select reading material outside the curriculum. For example, the recommended reading list provided in the *LANGUAGE! Teacher Resource Guide* includes the Lexile text measure for each suggested selection. For independent reading, students should select material 250L below their assessed Lexile measure. Students should be able to read and understand this level of material independently.

Communicate with parents meaningfully. Teachers can use the LRS data to provide specific information about their child's reading comprehension status and progress. For example, a teacher might say: "Your child will be able to read with at least 75% comprehension these kinds of materials which are at the next grade level." Or, "Your child will need to be able to increase his/her Lexile® measure by 400-500 Lexile points in the next few years to be prepared for college reading demands. Here is a list of appropriate titles your child can choose from for reading this summer."

Evaluating Growth Between Baseline and Progress Indicator

This section describes how to interpret growth for the LRS. Because the Baseline test and the Progress Indicator test use alternate test forms (A and B), raw scores should not be compared across test forms. To evaluate whether a student has changed their relative standing in the national normative sample for the test, changes in Lexile measures must be examined.

To begin, consider the amount of growth observed for a typical student over a year—the 50th percentile reader. We can assume that the general amount of measurement error for the LRS is 55 Lexile points. How long will it take for the typical student's reading level to grow before a difference is significant? In order for the difference between two reading measurements (beginning and end) to be significant, they must differ by more than 110L (two times the measurement error).

The table below shows the expected Lexile growth over the course of one year.

Grade	Expected Growth During One Year	Estimated Amount Per Week (36 weeks)	Instructional Time Necessary to Observe a "True" Difference
2	300L	8L	14 weeks
3	100L	3L	37 weeks
4	100L	3L	37 weeks
5	100L	3L	37 weeks
6	70L	2L	55 weeks
7	70L	2L	55 weeks
8	50L	1L	110 weeks
9	50L	1L	110 weeks
10	25L	1L	110 weeks
11	25L	1L	110 weeks

The chart above shows typical amount of growth for an average 50th percentile reader in a particular grade. In order to improve their performance up to average levels, students enrolled in *LANGUAGE!* need to demonstrate accelerated growth; that is, they need to show growth that exceeds the amounts shown in the chart for the grade the student is in. For example, a student in 7th grade is expected to gain 70L for a year of instruction. A Lexile measure gain of 100L would suggest an acceleration of learning because it exceeds the expected growth for typical 7th graders.

LRS Scoring Key

Baseline Form A

1. d
2. b
3. b
4. c
5. a
6. a
7. b
8. a
9. a
10. d
11. d
12. c
13. b
14. b
15. d
16. b
17. a
18. c
19. a
20. c
21. d
22. d
23. c
24. c
25. b
26. a
27. a
28. c
29. b
30. a
31. b
32. c
33. b
34. d
35. d
36. d
37. c
38. d
39. a
40. b
41. b
42. c
43. c
44. d
45. c
46. a
47. c
48. d
49. b

Progress Indicator Form B

1. c
2. d
3. a
4. c
5. b
6. b
7. a
8. a
9. b
10. a
11. d
12. c
13. d
14. b
15. b
16. d
17. d
18. b
19. c
20. d
21. a
22. a
23. c
24. c
25. b
26. a
27. a
28. b
29. d
30. a
31. a
32. c
33. b
34. b
35. d
36. c
37. c
38. b
39. a
40. a
41. d
42. d
43. b
44. d
45. c
46. d
47. a
48. b
49. c

Converting LRS Raw Scores to Lexile® Measures for Book A

Converting LRS Forms A and B Raw Scores to Lexile Measures		
Baseline Form A		Progress Indicator Form B
Reported Lexile Measure for Form A	Raw Score for Form A or Form B	Reported Lexile Measure for Form B
BR	0	BR
BR	1	BR
BR	2	BR
BR	3	BR
BR	4	BR
BR	5	BR
BR	6	BR
BR	7	BR
BR	8	BR
BR	9	BR
BR	10	BR
BR	11	BR
BR	12	BR
BR	13	10L
BR	14	30L
BR	15	50L
BR	16	70L
15L	17	90L
35L	18	110L
55L	19	130L
70L	20	150L
90L	21	165L
105L	22	185L
125L	23	205L
140L	24	220L
160L	25	240L
175L	26	255L
195L	27	275L
210L	28	290L
230L	29	310L
250L	30	330L

(Continued on next page)

Readers who score below 0L receive a score of BR (Beginner Reader). BR scores can be used for selecting books, planning instruction, and sharing results with parents. To evaluate students' growth, convert BR scores to actual (research) Lexile measures using the conversion table on page 91.

Baseline Assessment and Progress Indicators

Baseline Form A		Progress Indicator Form B
Reported Lexile Measure for Form A	Raw Score for Form A or Form B	Reported Lexile Measure for Form B
265L	31	350L
285L	32	365L
305L	33	385L
325L	34	405L
345L	35	430L
365L	36	450L
390L	37	475L
410L	38	495L
435L	39	520L
465L	40	550L
490L	41	580L
525L	42	610L
560L	43	645L
600L	44	690L
645L	45	735L
705L	46	795L
705L	47	795L
705L	48	795L
705L	49	795L

Converting LRS Forms A and B BR Lexile Scores to Research Lexile Measures for Book A				
Baseline Form A			Progress Indicator Form B	
Reported Lexile Measure	Research Lexile Measure	Raw Score for Form A or Form B	Research Lexile Measure	Reported Lexile Measure
BR	-841	0	-770	BR
BR	-621	1	-549	BR
BR	-488	2	-416	BR
BR	-407	3	-335	BR
BR	-347	4	-275	BR
BR	-300	5	-227	BR
BR	-259	6	-186	BR
BR	-224	7	-150	BR
BR	-192	8	-118	BR
BR	-163	9	-89	BR
BR	-136	10	-62	BR
BR	-111	11	-37	BR
BR	-88	12	-13	BR
BR	-65	13		
BR	-44	14		
BR	-23	15		
BR	-3	16		

Use this table to convert BR Lexile scores to actual Lexile scores for evaluation and research purposes. BR scores correspond to negative Lexile values. Educators should never share negative Lexile scores with students. Use BR for selecting books, planning instruction, and sharing results with parents.

Test of Written Spelling, Fourth Edition (TWS-4)

Description of the TWS-4

The TWS-4 is a norm-referenced test of spelling. It has two equivalent forms. The test is administered using a dictated word format. The test was normed on a large sample of students in Grades 1 through 12. Appropriate demographic characteristics of the sample were keyed to similar demographic characteristics of the United States population in 1990 and to those projected for the year 2000 (U.S. Bureau of the Census, 1997). Test results are reported as standard scores, percentiles, and grade equivalents. In addition to being extensively normed, the TWS-4 also has consistently high reliability and a demonstrated high degree of validity. This last feature is particularly noteworthy because it demonstrates that the TWS-4 does indeed measure written spelling.

Also, special procedures were used to show that the TWS-4 items are relatively free of bias. Readers interested in specific details pertaining to norming, item selection, validity, reliability and bias should see the TWS-4 Examiner's Manual (Larson, Hammill, Moats, 1999).

Most other commercially-produced spelling tests use a testing format that does not require the student to write even a single word. An example of such "proof-spelling" test formats is to ask the student to look at five words, only one of which is spelled correctly (e.g., *girlz, peice, freeze, flowre, tabel*). The student is to indicate the one that is correctly spelled. This type of format, while helpful in determining which students may be capable of editing spelling errors in a written product, will not indicate proficiency in the writing of words without a visual stimulus. The TWS-4, by using a dictated-word test procedure, can be expected to yield a more valid estimate of how well an student can actually spell words in written form.

When using the TWS-4 to document progress, one will want to supplement a test of this kind with criterion-referenced, informal measures that directly measure the specific skills the child might have learned; children may make progress in the sense of knowing more words but may not change their level of relative standing (standard score or percentile rank). For example, *Words Their Way* (Bear, Invernizzi, Templeton, and Johnston, 2000) contains specific word lists and criterion tests.

Administration and Scoring Procedures

This section explains how to administer and score the TWS-4. The discussion includes (a) basic testing procedures, (b) rules governing basals, ceilings, and scoring, and (c) specific instructions for administering the TWS-4.

Basic Testing Procedures

The chart below shows which TWS-4 forms should be used for the Baseline and Progress Indicator tests.

	Baseline	Progress Indicator
Test Form	Student *Baseline and Summative Assessment* booklet, Form A, page 21	Student *Baseline and Summative Assessment* booklet, Form B, page 55
When to administer	Before Unit 1	Unit 6

The examiner can assure a reliable administration of the test by adhering to several simple rules:

1. Become thoroughly familiar with the contents of this section.
2. Practice administering the test to an individual student no fewer than three times.
3. Allow about 15 minutes to administer the TWS-4. A slightly longer time period may be required when the test is administered in a group setting.

Basals, Ceilings, and Scoring

When administering the TWS-4 to an individual, the teacher should begin testing at the appropriate entry level and test until a ceiling is achieved or until the final item is administered. The ceiling is that point at which the student misses five consecutive items. If for some reason items above the ceiling were administered and a few were passed, the "passed" items are to be scored as incorrect. *Remember that all items above the ceiling are scored as incorrect.*

The following entry points are used for both individual and group administration of the TWS-4:

Entry Level by *LANGUAGE!* Book

Books A and B: Item 1

Books C and D: Item 10

Books E and F: Item 20

For Books C through F, once a ceiling has been established, the teacher should go back and establish a basal if the student has not already answered five consecutive items correctly. That is, if the student did not correctly answer five items in succession during the establishment of a ceiling, the teacher should return to the entry point and test downward until five items in a row are answered correctly or until Item 1 has been administered. *All items below the basal are scored as correct.*

For Books A and B, the teacher does not need to go back and establish a basal because the entry point is item 1.

The proper use of basals and ceilings is illustrated in Figure 4.6. The three examples pertain to the scoring of the test when administered to a student in Book E who is 13 years and 6 months of age. In Example A, the teacher began by introducing Item 20 because the student was in Book E. Progressively higher numbered (and increasingly more difficult) items were given until the student missed five in a row (the ceiling, Item 34). The teacher returned to Item 20 and began testing downward until five items in a row were answered correctly (the basal, Item 13). At this point testing was discontinued, the correct items were added, credit was given for the items unadministered below the basal, and the total raw score (23) was recorded in the appropriate space.

In Example B, the teacher also began testing with Item 20, which was missed by the student. Testing proceeded upward until the ceiling was achieved (Item 28), at which point the teacher moved to Item 19 and tested downward. Because no basal was achieved, all of the items, including Item 1, were administered. This situation occurs frequently in the testing of young students who are weak in spelling. All correct responses were summed and the total (18) properly recorded.

In Example C, for some unexplained reason, all of the items on the subtest were improperly administered, including items below the basal and above the ceiling. In these cases, the subtest is always scored as if the basal or ceiling had been attained in the proper fashion. In Example C, the student is credited with the first 20 items and with Items 23 and 24. The total raw score is 22. Even though the student "passed" Items 30 and 32, no credit is given because the items are above the ceiling. Additionally, although the student "failed" Item 15, credit is given because the item falls below the basal.

When testing groups of students, the teacher should attempt to administer enough items to ensure that the students achieve basals and ceilings. After scoring, the teacher will find that some students did not achieve basals and ceilings. These students are to be taken aside individually and administered additional items until proper basals and ceilings are reached. Scoring the TWS-4 is quite simple, because the words written by the student(s) are merely scored as correct or incorrect. Correct responses earn 1 point while incorrect responses receive no credit. The number of correct items is summed, and this value is the raw score. No qualitative scoring judgments are required of the teacher. Unreadable words should be rewritten by the student.

Example A						Example B					Example C					
1.			26.	1		1.	1	26.	0		1.	1		26.	0	
2.			27.	0		2.	1	27.	0		2.	1		27.	0	
3.			28.	1		3.	0	28.	0		3.	1		28.	0	
4.			29.	1		4.	1	29.			4.	1		29.	0	
5.			30.	0		5.	1	30.			5.	1		30.	1	
6.		+12	31.	0		6.	1	31.			6.	1		31.	0	
7.			32.	0		7.	1	32.			7.	1		32.	1	
8.			33.	0		8.	0	33.			8.	1	+15	33.	0	
9.			34.	0		9.	1	34.			9.	1		34.	0	
10.			35.			10.	1	35.			10.	1		35.	0	
11.			36.			11.	1	36.			11.	1		36.	0	
12.			37.			12.	0	37.			12.	1		37.	0	
13.	1		38.			13.	1	38.			13.	1		38.	0	
14.	1		39.			14.	1	39.		+0	14.	1		39.	0	+0
15.	1		40.			15.	1	40.			15.	0		40.	0	
16.	1		41.			16.	1	41.			16.	1		41.	0	
17.	1		42.		+0	17.	0	42.			17.	1		42.	0	
18.	0		43.			18.	1	43.			18.	1		43.	0	
19.	0		44.			19.	1	44.			19.	1		44.	0	
20.	1		45.			20.	0	45.			20.	1		45.	0	
21.	1		46.			21.	1	46.			21.	0		46.	0	
22.	0		47.			22.	1	47.			22.	0		47.	0	
23.	1		48.			23.	1	48.			23.	1		48.	0	
24.	0		49.			24.	0	49.			24.	1		49.	0	
25.	0		50.			25.	0	50.			25.	0		50.	0	
Total Raw Score	23					Total Raw Score	18				Total Raw Score	22				

Figure 4.6. Proper use of basals and ceilings

Specific Administration Instructions

When administering the TWS-4 to an individual or to a group, the teacher should keep several points firmly in mind. Because students are required to write the words dictated by the teacher, they must be seated in a comfortable position and be given adequate time to respond to the presentation of the words. The words are sequenced in order of difficulty and should be presented in such a fashion that the students are not unnecessarily bored or frustrated.

When administering the TWS-4 to an individual, the teacher must monitor the performance of the student continuously and terminate testing when *five consecutive errors* are made. When administering the TWS-4 to a group of students (e.g., an entire class), specific monitoring of an individual student's performance will be very difficult, if not impossible. For this reason, some criteria must be set for the total number of words to be administered to students of differing ages in order to avoid undue frustration.

Use the following guidelines:

- Groups of students in Books A and B should be required to spell the first 20 words.
- Groups of students in Books C and D should begin with Item 10 and conclude with Item 30.
- Groups of students in Books E and F should be asked to spell Items 20 through 50.

Teachers should remember to apply the rules governing basals and ceilings when scoring group-administered tests. This means that some individuals will have to be tested individually until they achieve the necessary basal or ceiling.

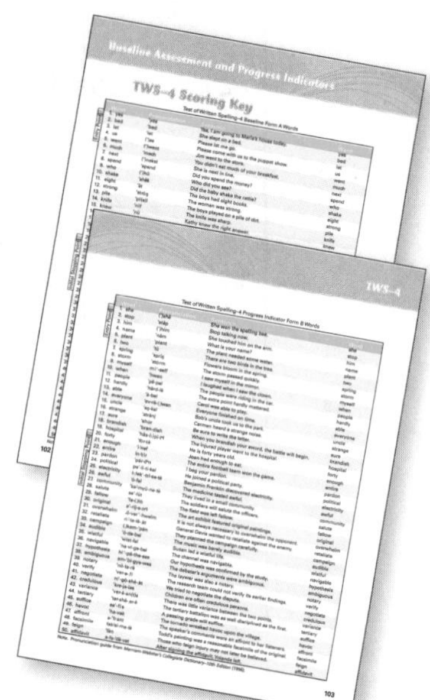

TWS-4 Scoring Key

The teacher should not hesitate to administer the TWS-4 in two or more sessions for young or immature students.

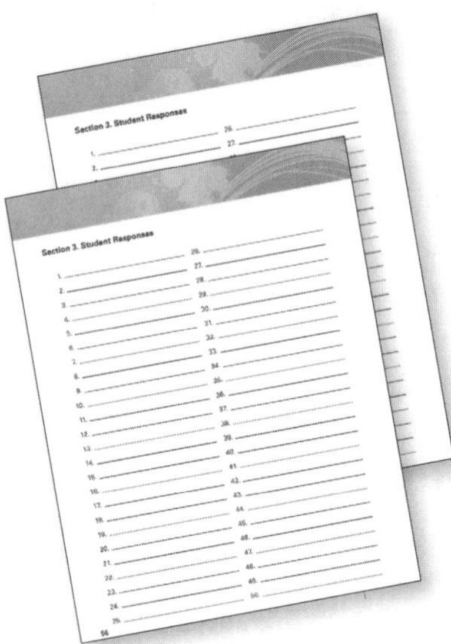

Section 3. Student Responses

Step 1: Before testing begins, locate the words and accompanying sentences, along with a key to the pronunciation symbols on page 102 for Baseline (Form A) or on page 103 for Progress Indicator (Form B) in this guide.

Step 2: Have students turn to page 22 for Baseline or page 56 for Progress Indicator in their *Baseline and Summative Assessment*, Book A, booklets. Check to see that students are on the correct page.

In administering the test, the teacher first says the word in isolation, then says the sentence that contains the word, and finally says the word in isolation again. The students write the words in their *Baseline and Summative Assessment*, Book A, booklets, page 22, section 3, for Baseline and page 56, section 3 for Progress Indicator.

Scoring the TWS-4

Score the test using the word list on page 102 of this guide for Baseline (Form A) or page 103 for Progress Indicator (Form B). The raw score is the total number of items answered correctly.

Interpreting the TWS-4 Results

This section presents information about interpreting the TWS-4 results.

The topics to be addressed include (a) how to record the scores, (b) how to interpret the scores and their relationship to ability strengths and weaknesses, (c) using student performance for instructional planning, and (d) how to evaluate growth between Baseline and Progress Indicator.

Recording of TWS-4 Scores

Converting raw scores to normative scores can happen in two ways: manually or by using the *Online Assessment System*. The *Online Assessment System* provides users with the normative scores listed in the table below. Without use of the *Online Assessment System* (manual recording of scores), only grade equivalents are provided.

Normative Scores Provided	
Online Assessment System	Manual
Converts raw scores to: • grade equivalents • percentile ranks • standard scores • descriptive ratings of standard scores	Converts raw scores to: • grade equivalents
Note: no need to use print record forms	Note: must use print record forms: TWS-4 Student Record Form, Summary Record Form, Baseline and Progress Indicator Class Roster.

Recording using the *LANGUAGE! Online Assessment System*

Enter raw scores into the *LANGUAGE! Online Assessment System*. The Web-based data entry and reporting system will convert raw scores to grade equivalents, percentile ranks and standard scores, and descriptive ratings of the tests' standard scores. Student birth date and test date must be entered in the online system to obtain standard scores and percentiles.

Detailed discussions of the normative scores are found in the "Test Scores and Their Interpretation" section of this chapter. The descriptive ratings of the standard scores are found in Table 4.7.

Manual Recording

Use the conversion table on page 104 to convert TWS-4 raw scores to grade equivalents. A detailed discussion of grade equivalents is found in the next section.

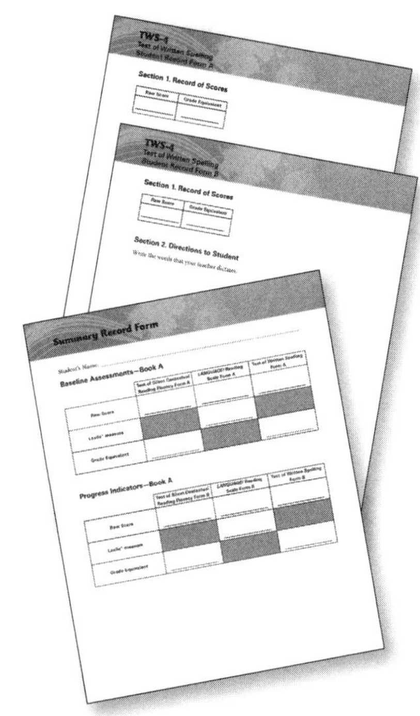

Once grade equivalents are obtained, scores should be recorded on the print record forms:

- **TWS-4 Student Record Form**—An individual's test performance is recorded on the TWS-4 Student Record Form in the student *Baseline and Summative Assessment* on page 21 for Baseline Form A and page 55 for Progress Indicator Form B.
- **Summary Record Form**—This form summarizes all Baseline and Summative assessment scores for an individual. This form can be found in the student *Baseline and Summative Assessment*, on page 61.
- **Baseline and Progress Indicator Class Roster**—This form summarizes all Baseline and Progress Indicator assessment scores (not including writing) for a class. Transfer scores from the students' Summary Record Forms to the Baseline and Progress Indicator Class Roster found in Appendix B.

Test Scores and Their Interpretation

The chart below shows the normative scores provided for TWS-4: raw scores, standard scores, percentile ranks, and grade equivalents. This section includes a brief discussion of each score and how it should be interpreted. The shortcomings of these scores and cautions about their use are also discussed.

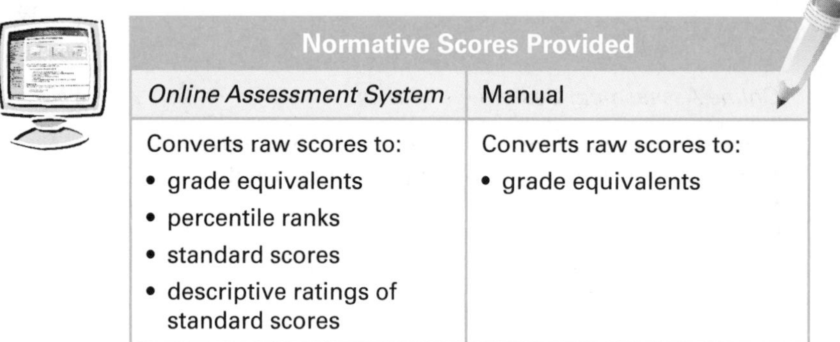

Normative Scores Provided	
Online Assessment System	Manual
Converts raw scores to: • grade equivalents • percentile ranks • standard scores • descriptive ratings of standard scores	Converts raw scores to: • grade equivalents

Raw Scores

Raw scores are the number of items scored correct on each test. These scores are useful only for generating normative scores, such as standard scores, percentiles, and grade equivalents.

Standard Scores

The clearest indication of a student's performance on the TWS-4 is provided by some type of standard score. This type of score provides a precise estimate of the extent to which the student's performance is different from the average of other students from the normative sample at the same age. It is suitable for comparing TWS-4 performance with Test of Silent Contextual Reading Fluency (TOSCRF) performance Lyman (1998) defined a standard score as "any of several derived scores based on the number of standard deviations between a given raw score and the mean of the distribution" (p. 160). The standard scores on the TWS-4 are derived from a distribution that has a mean of 100 and a standard deviation of 15. Guidelines for interpreting standard scores are provided in Table 4.7.

Raw scores are converted to standard scores using the *LANGUAGE! Online Assessment System*. To obtain standard scores, raw scores along with the date on which the student was tested and birth date must be entered into the *LANGUAGE! Online Assessment System*.

Table 4.7

Standard Score	Description	% Included
>130	Very superior	2.34
121–130	Superior	6.87
111–120	Above average	16.12
90–110	Average	49.51
80–89	Below average	16.12
70–79	Poor	6.87
<70	Very poor	2.34

Percentile Ranks

Percentile ranks indicate the percentage of the distribution that is equal to or below a particular score. For example, a percentile rank of 65 of the age 13 years and 4 months means that 65% of the standardization sample at that age scored at or below the student's score. Because this interpretation is easy to understand, percentile ranks are often used by practitioners when sharing test results with others. The distance between two percentile ranks increases as they move farther from the mean or average (i.e., the 50th percentile). Therefore, percentile ranks cannot be arithmetically manipulated (e.g., by adding, subtracting, or averaging the scores) in the same manner as standard scores. Although percentile ranks are convenient and popular, examiners should be familiar with their advantages and disadvantages as explained by Aiken (2000), McLoughlin and Lewis (2001), and Salvia and Ysseldyke (2001).

Raw scores are converted to percentile ranks using the *LANGUAGE! Online Assessment System*. To obtain percentiles, raw scores along with the date on which the student was tested and birth date must be entered into the *LANGUAGE! Online Assessment System*.

Grade Equivalents

Grade equivalents for tests are usually labeled according to the content of the test. Thus, grade equivalents associated with tests of spelling are called "spelling grade levels."

Raw scores are converted to grade equivalents using the *LANGUAGE! Online Assessment System* or the conversion table.

For example, a raw score of 18 translates into a grade equivalent of 4.2 in the table on page 104. A grade equivalent of 4.2 indicates that the student's performance is similar to that of students in the normative sample who were in the 2nd month of the 4th grade.

The TWS-4 spelling grade equivalents are derived by calculating the average score of students in the normative group at each school grade. For example, the average score of students in fourth grade is 17 items correct; any student obtaining a score of 17 receives a grade equivalent of 4.0. Through a process of interpolation, extrapolation, and smoothing, spelling grade equivalents are generated for each raw score point achieved on the TWS-4 total score.

Because interpolation, extrapolation, and smoothing are used to create grade equivalents, they should always be interpreted with caution. We provide them, reluctantly, only because some state and local policies require these types of scores. We urge TWS-4 users to read the concerns expressed by Aiken (2000), Anastasi and Urbina (1997), Linn and Miller (2005), and Salvia and Ysseldyke (2001) regarding the use of grade equivalents. The arguments against these scores focused on the fact that they are frequently misunderstood, have limited value statistically, require a good deal of subjective interpolation to calculate, and often give an unrealistic picture of a youngster's true abilities. We prefer that TWS-4 users employ standard scores or percentiles when possible.

Using Student Performance Results for Instructional Planning

The interpretation of the TWS-4 scores focuses upon percentiles and standard scores. Teachers and diagnosticians should be concerned when a student's standard score is below 90. This means the student is such a poor speller that special attention is probably necessary or additional assessment may be needed to specify the cause for such a serious problem (e.g., low intelligence, auditory/visual difficulties, lack of instruction). Students who score in the 90 to 110 range are performing at an expected level for their age. Those scoring over 110 excel in spelling; they have mastered basic spelling patterns of English orthography and are likely to be proficient readers and writers as well.

Obtaining a standard score with a measure such as the TWS-4 is only one meaningful way to examine spelling and its possible link to a learning disability. Others include informal error analysis, criterion-referenced testing, and informal sampling of very specific skills that will be targeted for instruction. Readers interested in specific details pertaining to supplement assessments of spelling and related skills should see Chapter 4 of the TWS-4 Examiner's Manual (Larson, Hammill, Moats, 1999) or *Words Their Way* (Bear, Invernizzi, Templeton, and Johnston, 2000).

When students who are in the *LANGUAGE!* curriculum show low performance on the TWS-4, there should be increased attention instructionally and more careful monitoring and analysis of performance on the Content Mastery and Fluency tasks in Steps 1 and 2. Content and skill development is targeted for improvement in spelling.

Step	Instructional focus
Step 1: Phonemic Awareness and Phonics	Emphasizes the basic sound-spelling correspondences needed to spell phonetically predictable words correctly. Instructional attention on phoneme, syllable, and morpheme awareness within words contributes to increased accuracy when spelling.
Step 2: Word Recognition and Spelling	Provides systematic practice applying sound-spelling correspondences. In addition to the spelling lists for each unit, the Unit Words in each unit provide an expanded list of words for additional spelling practice. The addition of inflectional endings and the rules governing how to correctly add them to base words is also a part of the instruction in Step 2. *LANGUAGE!* also systematically develops accurate spelling of high frequency, non-phonetic words through the Essential Words in each unit.

For further elaboration on the content of each Step in *LANGUAGE!*, turn to the *Teacher Resource Guide* for information on each Step of the instructional lesson.

Evaluating Growth Between Baseline and Progress Indicator

This section describes how to interpret growth for the TWS-4. To evaluate whether a student has changed their relative standing in the national normative sample for the test, changes in standard scores (using the *Online Assessment System*) or grade equivalents must be examined.

Note: Because Baseline and Progress Indicators use alternate test forms (A and B), raw scores should not be compared across test forms.

Evaluating Growth Using Standard Scores

Standard scores show relative standing compared to others in the national normative sample for the test. A student must demonstrate a certain amount of growth in raw score to maintain his or her standard score (i.e., relative standing in the norming group).

To examine whether a student is improving her relative standing in the larger norming group for the test, examine the change in the student's standard score between the beginning of book (Baseline) and the end-of-book (Progress Indicator) assessment.

To understand how to evaluate growth using standard scores, note the following:

- An increase in a student's raw score does not necessarily mean an improvement in her standard score. For example, consider a student achieves a standard score on the Baseline test of 100, which represents the 50th percentile for any student age group. The student's raw score must improve relative to the norming sample at the student's age at the time of the Progress Indicator test in order to maintain a standard score of 100.
- When a student's standard score stay the same from Baseline to Progress Indicator, then she is maintaining her relative standing in the norming group. Students who maintain their relative standing (i.e., show no change in standard score) from year to year are showing an improvement in raw score performance.
- When a student's standard score increases from Baseline to Progress Indicator, then she is improving her relative standing in the norming group.
- When a student's standard score decline from Baseline to Progress Indicator, she is losing her relative standing in the norming group. This means that her raw score performance over the instructional period is either increasing (by an insufficient amount to register a standard score gain), staying the same, or declining.

Evaluating Growth Using Grade Equivalents

Grade equivalents represent the average score of students in the normative group for the test at each school grade.

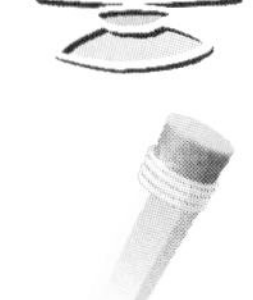

To understand how to evaluate growth using grade equivalents, note the following:

- When a student's grade equivalent score increases between Baseline and Progress Indicator, the student is showing growth.
- The interpretation of an increase (or decrease) in grade equivalents depends on the size of increase.
- If the change in grade equivalent between Baseline and Progress Indicator is equal to the actual number of months in the school year that have passed, then the gain reflects a rate of growth that is expected based on average development.
- If the grade equivalent gain exceeds the number of months that have actually passed, then the gain reflects a rate of growth that is accelerated; that is, the gain exceeds a rate of growth that would be expected for average development.

TWS-4 Words for Baseline Form A

	Word	Pronunciation	Sentence	Word
Entry Point	1. yes	'yes	Yes, I am going to Maria's house today.	yes
	2. bed	'bed	She slept on a bed.	bed
	3. let	'let	Please let me go.	let
	4. us	(')əs	Please come with us to the puppet show.	us
	5. went	(')went	Jim went to the store.	went
	6. much	'məch	You didn't eat much of your breakfast.	much
	7. next	(')nekst	She is next in line.	next
	8. spend	'spend	Did you spend the money?	spend
	9. who	(')hü	Who did you see?	who
	10. shake	'shāk	Did the baby shake the rattle?	shake
	11. eight	'āt	The boys had eight books.	eight
	12. strong	'strȯŋ	The woman was strong.	strong
	13. pile	'pī(ə)l	The boys played on a pile of dirt.	pile
	14. knife	'nīf	The knife was sharp.	knife
	15. knew	'nü	Kathy knew the right answer.	knew
	16. tardy	'tär-dē	Alan was tardy for school.	tardy
	17. nineteen	(')nīn-'tēn	My brother is nineteen years old.	nineteen
	18. section	'sek-shən	The farmers worked one section of land.	section
	19. signal	'sig-nᵊl	The cars stopped at the traffic signal.	signal
Initial Stopping Point	20. expect	ik'-spekt	We expect them to be on time.	expect
	21. canyon	'kan-yən	The canyon is very deep.	canyon
	22. district	'dis-(ˌ)trikt	The congressman campaigned in his district.	district
	23. fountain	'fau̇n-tᵊn	There was water in the fountain.	fountain
	24. legal	'lē-gəl	The judge has legal authority.	legal
	25. terrible	'ter-ə-bəl	Dorothy saw the terrible storm.	terrible
	26. unify	'yü-nə-ˌfī	Discord does little to unify a group.	unify
	27. bicycle	'bī-ˌsi-kəl	Paul received a bicycle for his birthday.	bicycle
	28. institution	ˌin(t)-stə'-tyü-shən	The school is sometimes called an institution of learning.	institution
	29. collar	'kä-lər	She buttoned her collar.	collar
	30. agriculture	'a-gri-ˌkəl-chər	Agriculture is an important part of the economy.	agriculture
	31. visualize	'vi-zhə-wə-ˌlīz	It is not always possible to visualize a dream.	visualize
	32. baste	'bāst	It's time to baste the turkey.	baste
	33. nucleus	'nyü-klē-əs	The returning lettermen form the nucleus of a strong team.	nucleus
	34. tangible	'tan-jə-bəl	No tangible results came from the survey.	tangible
	35. tranquil	'traŋ-kwəl	The tranquil scene helped calm her thoughts.	tranquil
	36. continuity	ˌkän-tᵊn-'ü-ə-tē	There is little continuity in the stock.	continuity
	37. luminous	'lü-mə-nəs	The luminous sign was an effective advertising tool.	luminous
	38. laborious	lə'-bor-ē-əs	The laborious task took four hours.	laborious
	39. linguistic	liŋ'-gwis-tik	John's linguistic competence was well recognized.	linguistic
	40. opaque	ō'-pāk	The new fingernail polish was opaque.	opaque
	41. gauntlet	'gȯnt-lət	The group had its new members run the gauntlet.	gauntlet
	42. panorama	ˌpa-nə'-ra-mə	The wall contained a panorama of the Grand Canyon.	panorama
	43. finesse	fə-'nes	The game of bridge requires finesse.	finesse
	44. gregarious	gri'-gar-ē-əs	Sheep are gregarious creatures.	gregarious
	45. zealous	'ze-ləs	Jose was zealous in his beliefs.	zealous
	46. requisite	're-kwə-zət	The student did not have the requisite skills for the course.	requisite
	47. champagne	sham'-pān	Champagne was used to toast the bride and groom.	champagne
	48. cyst	'sist	A cyst was found in the dog's leg.	cyst
	49. versatile	'vər-sə-tᵊl	Susan was a very versatile dancer.	versatile
	50. liaison	'lē-ə-ˌzän	The company's liaison spoke to the general.	liaison

Note: Pronunciation guide from *Merriam-Webster's Collegiate Dictionary–10th Edition* (1996).

TWS-4 Words for Progress Indicator Form B

	Word	Pronunciation	Sentence	Word
Entry Point	1. she	(ˈ)shē	She won the spelling bee.	she
	2. stop	ˈstäp	Stop talking now.	stop
	3. him	(ˈ)him	She touched him on the arm.	him
	4. name	ˈnām	What is your name?	name
	5. plant	ˈplant	The plant needed some water.	plant
	6. two	ˈtü	There are two birds in the tree.	two
	7. spring	ˈspriŋ	Flowers bloom in the spring.	spring
	8. storm	ˈstȯrm	The storm passed quickly.	storm
	9. myself	mīˈ-self	I saw myself in the mirror.	myself
	10. when	ˈhwen	I laughed when I saw the clown.	when
	11. people	ˈpē-pəl	The people were riding in the car.	people
	12. hardly	ˈhärd-lē	The extra point hardly mattered.	hardly
	13. able	ˈā-bəl	Carol was able to play.	able
	14. everyone	ˈev-rē-(ˌ)wən	Everyone finished on time.	everyone
	15. uncle	ˈəŋ-kəl	Bob's uncle took us to the park.	uncle
	16. strange	ˈstrānj	Carmen heard a strange noise.	strange
	17. sure	ˈshu̇r	Be sure to write the letter.	sure
	18. brandish	ˈbran-dish	When you brandish your sword, the battle will begin.	brandish
	19. hospital	ˈhäs-(ˌ)pi-tᵊl	The injured player went to the hospital.	hospital
Initial Stopping Point	20. forty	ˈfȯr-tē	He is forty years old.	forty
	21. enough	i-ˈnəf	Joan had enough to eat.	enough
	22. entire	in-ˈtīr	The entire football team won the game.	entire
	23. pardon	ˈpär-dᵊn	I beg your pardon.	pardon
	24. political	pəˈ-li-ti-kəl	He joined a political party.	political
	25. electricity	i-ˌlekˈ-tri-sə-tē	Benjamin Franklin discovered electricity.	electricity
	26. awful	ˈȯ-fəl	The medicine tasted awful.	awful
	27. community	ˈkə-ˈmyü-nə-tē	They lived in a small community.	community
	28. salute	səˈ-lüt	The soldiers will salute the officers.	salute
	29. fallow	ˈfa-(ˌ)lō	The field was left fallow.	fallow
	30. original	əˈ-rij-ə-nᵊl	The art exhibit featured original paintings.	original
	31. overwhelm	ˌō-vərˈ-hwelm	It is not always necessary to overwhelm the opponent.	overwhelm
	32. retaliate	ri-ˈta-lē-ˌāt	General Davis wanted to retaliate against the enemy.	retaliate
	33. campaign	(ˌ)kam-ˈpān	They planned the campaign carefully.	campaign
	34. audible	ˈȯ-də-bəl	The music was barely audible.	audible
	35. wistful	ˈwist-fəl	Susan led a wistful life.	wistful
	36. navigable	ˈna-vi-gə-bəl	The channel was navigable.	navigable
	37. hypothesis	hīˈ-pä-thə-səs	Our hypothesis was confirmed by the study.	hypothesis
	38. ambiguous	am-ˈbi-gyə-wəs	The debater's arguments were ambiguous.	ambiguous
	39. notary	ˈnō-tə-rē	The laywer was also a notary.	notary
	40. verify	ˈver-ə-ˌfī	The research team could not verify its earlier findings.	verify
	41. negotiate	niˈ-gō-shē-ˌāt	We tried to negotiate the dispute.	negotiate
	42. credulous	ˈkre-jə-ləs	Children are often credulous persons.	credulous
	43. variance	ˈver-ē-ən(t)s	There was little variance between the two points.	variance
	44. tertiary	ˈtər-shē-ˌer-ē	The tertiary battalion was as well disciplined as the first.	tertiary
	45. suffice	səˈ-fīs	A passing grade will suffice.	suffice
	46. havoc	ˈha-vək	The tornado wreaked havoc upon the village.	havoc
	47. affront	ə-ˈfrənt	The speaker's comments were an affront to her listeners.	affront
	48. facsimile	fak-ˈsi-mə-lē	Todd's painting was a reasonable facsimile of the original.	facsimile
	49. feign	ˈfān	Those who feign injury may not later be believed.	feign
	50. affidavit	ˌa-fə-ˈdā-vət	After signing the affidavit, Yolanda left.	affidavit

Note: Pronunciation guide from *Merriam-Webster's Collegiate Dictionary–10th Edition* (1996).

Converting TWS-4 Baseline Form A and Progress Indicator Form B Raw Scores to Grade Equivalents for Book A

Raw Score for Form A or B	Grade Equivalent
<5	<1.0
5	1.0
6	1.2
7	1.4
8	1.7
9	2.0
10	2.2
11	2.4
12	2.7
13	3.0
14	3.2
15	3.4
16	3.7
17	4.0
18	4.2
19	4.4

Raw Score for Form A or B	Grade Equivalent
20	4.7
21–22	5.0
23	5.2
24	5.4
25	5.7
26	6.2
27	6.7
28	7.0
29	7.4
30	8.4
31	9.4
32	10.4
33	11.4
34	12.4
>34	>12.4

Writing

Description of the Writing Test

The writing assessment in *LANGUAGE!* is designed to allow students to demonstrate what they already know about written expression (Baseline prompt) and how well they can apply what they have learned (Progress Indicator prompts). The purpose of collecting the Baseline writing sample is to assess students' strengths and weaknesses in written expression prior to beginning work in Book A. The purpose of collecting the Progress Indicator writing sample is to assess to what extent students have mastered the skills taught in Book A under the umbrella of the Six Traits of Effective Writing. The writing prompts for the Baseline and Progress Indicator samples are tailored to the type of writing students do within the book. In Book A, instruction focuses principally on the elements of an expository paragraph. Therefore, the prompt for Book A asks students to write a well-constructed paragraph.

Administration and Scoring Procedures

Before Administering the Prompt

- Make sure students have sharpened pencils with erasers.
- Provide paper for students to organize their ideas before they begin to write.
- Make sure each student has a *Summative Assessment* student book.
- Have dictionaries and thesauri available for students to use.

Administering the Writing Prompt

- Ask students to turn to page 23 of the *Summative Assessment* student book for the Baseline prompt (prior to beginning Book A instruction) or page 57 for the Progress Indicator prompt (upon completion of Book A instruction.)
- Read the prompt aloud to the students and review the criteria by which their paragraphs will be scored.
- Direct students to organize their thoughts on the sheet of paper you have provided for them. After they have done so, remind them to write their paragraphs in the *Summative Assessment* student book. They will have a total of 45 minutes to complete their work.
- Tell students to reread their paragraphs when they have finished writing and make any necessary revisions or corrections, keeping in mind the criteria by which their paragraphs will be scored. Encourage them to consult a dictionary or thesaurus to check their word choice and their spelling.

Summative Assessment
Student Book
Baseline Test, Page 23

Assessment: TE, Book A
Baseline test, Page 110

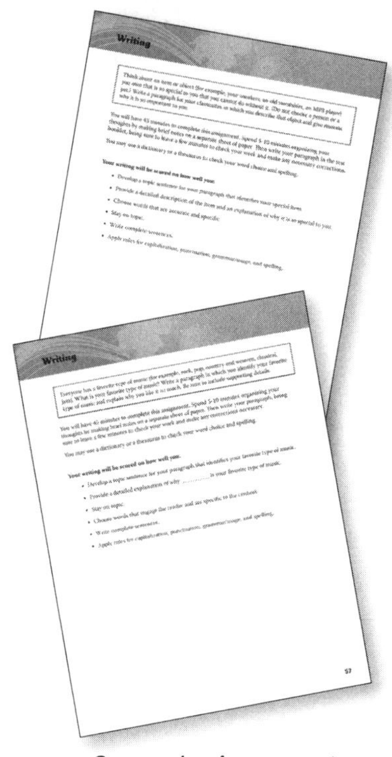

Summative Assessment
Student Book
Progress Indicator Test,
Page 57

Assessment: TE, Book A
Progress Indicator, Page 116

- Do not make specific comments on the content or mechanics of students' papers as they write. It is important that students demonstrate what they can do on their own, without the assistance of teachers or peers.
- At the conclusion of the testing period, collect students' *Summative Assessment* books, along with any notes they made on the paper you provided for them.

Universal Access

- If a student has a 504 plan or an Individualized Education Plan that calls for accommodations (such as using a scribe, for instance) when completing a written test, make sure the accommodations are in place during the administration of the writing sample.

Scoring Student Papers

- You will use a trait scoring approach to evaluate students' responses to the writing prompt and judge each student's work in the context of the Six Traits of Effective Writing, assigning a rating of 4, 3, 2, or 1 for each of the traits. If you are new to trait scoring, you may find it helpful to work with another teacher and rate a few papers together before working individually on the task.

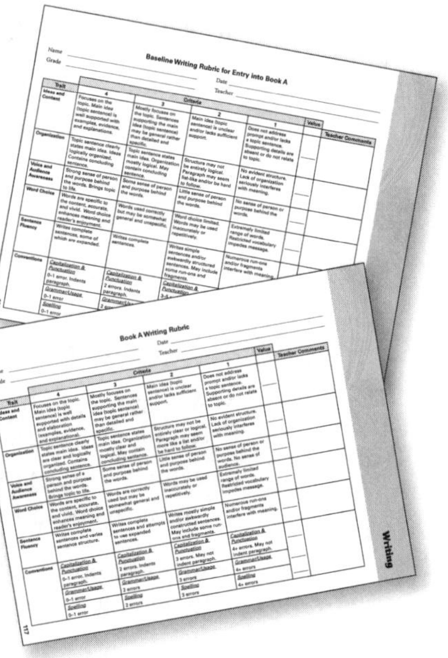

Baseline Writing Rubric for Entry into Book A

Book A Writing Rubric

- To rate Baseline papers, duplicate the Baseline Writing Rubric for Entry into Book A from the Book A *Instructional Planning Tools* CD. To rate Progress Indicator papers, duplicate the Book A Writing Rubric from the Book A *Instructional Planning Tools* CD. Attach a rubric to each student's writing sample.
- It is important to remember that the Six Traits of Effective Writing are not always distinct from one another. For instance, spelling performance in the Conventions category is easily classified as correct or incorrect and does not overlap in content with other traits. Voice and Audience Awareness, however, is more subjective and draws upon several traits. Therefore Voice and Audience Awareness is less easily rated.
- Read the sample student responses, as well as the commentaries, six-trait rating charts, and rating interpretations that accompany them. This material highlights a range of possible student responses and familiarizes you with the characteristics associated with a 4, 3, 2, or 1 rating for each of the six traits. For example, a 4 rating on the Organization trait indicates a student's performance matches (or nearly matches) the description in that cell of the rubric. At the other end of the scale, a 1 in Organization signals that the student has little or no facility in organizing his or her thoughts.

The student papers have been presented in order of their overall proficiency. You will notice that the Rating Interpretation below the Writing: Rating Summary form provides a global descriptor of the student's performance. For example, if a student earns mostly 4's on the six traits, the global descriptor is "Proficient." If the student earns mostly 3's, the descriptor is "Developing Proficiency." A paper with a preponderance of 2's demonstrates "Emerging Proficiency," while a paper with mostly 1's is "Not Proficient." (These terms are used only as a rationale for arranging the students' papers in a particular order and are not part of the writing assessment process. Writing assessment in *LANGUAGE!* focuses on students acquiring proficiency in the individual traits of effective writing rather than on a holistic rating.)

- After you have acquainted yourself with the student responses and their scoring, rate your students' paragraphs, using the appropriate rubric. Follow these steps:

  1) Read the student's paragraph in its entirety once, without stopping. This will give you a feel for the paper as a whole and permit a more accurate rating for Voice and Audience Awareness, a trait influenced by a number of factors.
  2) Reread the paragraph, assigning a numerical score to each trait. You may use a plus or minus in addition to the number if the student's work does not fit neatly into the description in a particular cell. You may also want to enter notes in the Teacher Comments column to help explain your rating, but this is not a requirement.
  3) Transfer the points for each trait to the Writing: Rating Summary section in the student's *Summative Assessment* book.
  4) Enter the rating information into the *LANGUAGE! Online Assessment System* to maintain an electronic record of performance for analysis in guiding instruction.
  5) Record all scores for a class on the print Baseline, Benchmark, and Progress Indicator Class Roster found in Appendix B.

Providing Feedback to Students

- *Sharing Baseline writing sample results with students:*

  When you have finished scoring the Baseline writing samples, arrange to have a conference with each student about the results. Begin by walking the student through the traits on which she or he did well, pointing explicitly to those parts of the paragraph. Next, discuss with the student areas of weakness, once again pointing explicitly to those areas of the paragraph. Ask the student to think about how he or she might improve the paper. If the student is unable to articulate any measures to take, you can offer suggestions yourself.

  Since this is a Baseline test, remind students that their performance is an indicator of where their skills in language expression currently stand. Upcoming instruction will help improve the areas of weakness this test has identified and build upon areas of strength. Let students know that they will have multiple opportunities throughout the course of instruction to improve and that their ratings on the two Benchmark papers and the final Progress Indicator writing sample will be compared to the Baseline rating to demonstrate growth.

- *Sharing Progress Indicator writing sample results with students:*

  When you have finished scoring the Progress Indicator writing samples, arrange to have a conference with each student about the results. Have on hand the student's writing sample and the Writing: Rating Summary form. The latter should contain the students' ratings for the Baseline test, the two Benchmark papers, and the final Progress Indicator writing sample. This is a time to promote students' pride in their accomplishments over the course of Book A. Start the conversation by discussing the Progress Indicator scores. Then ask students to compare the results from this test to the results from the Baseline and Benchmark measures. Prompt the student to verbalize his or her own growth from test to test. On which traits has the student improved his or her performance? What areas still need work? In the sample Rating Summary below, the student should be able to identify growth in all six traits, but especially in Organization, Word Choice, and Conventions. This student's goals going forward might be to work on Ideas and Content, Voice and Audience Awareness, or Sentence Fluency. Intense work on Sentence Fluency alone may, as a by-product, promote growth in Ideas and Content and Voice and Audience Awareness.

Writing: Rating Summary

Trait	Baseline	Benchmark (Unit 2)	Benchmark (Unit 4)	Progress Indicator
Ideas and Content	2	2	3	3
Organization	2	3	3	4
Voice and Audience Awareness	2	2	2	3
Word Choice	1	2	2	3
Sentence Fluency	2	2	3	3
Conventions				
Capitalization & Punctuation	1	2	3	4
Grammar/Usage	1	2	2	3
*Spelling**	1	2	3	4
Date Rated:	9/7/07	10/19/07	11/30/07	1/25/08

Using Student Performance Results for Instructional Planning

- *Using student scores to inform classroom instruction:*

  Examine the aggregated data on each of the six traits for your class, and look for patterns. If, for instance, most of the students scored low on Organization and high on Ideas and Content, you will want to weight classroom instruction and classroom time more toward Organization as they progress into the next book.

- *Using student scores to inform individual instruction:*

  If an examination of the class's aggregated scores reveals a few students who are deficient in a particular skill, there are many built-in opportunities in *LANGUAGE!* to address those weaknesses on a small-group or individual basis. You can turn to homework options, the Special Instructional Support material, or the If/Then boxes to provide additional practice in critical skills areas.

- *Using student scores to target instruction tied to the Six Traits of Effective writing:*

  Throughout the *LANGUAGE!* curriculum, students evaluate their own work using Writer's Checklists, while teachers evaluate students' writing with book-specific rubrics. Both of these instruments are linked to the Six Traits of Effective Writing. Instructional emphasis in the six steps of the instructional process contributes to improvement in these traits. The following table highlights some of the instruction-to-trait connections.

Trait	Instructional response in *LANGUAGE!*
Ideas and Content	Stress interpreting the writing prompt and using the reading material and other sources to gather and organize information. (Step 5)
Organization	Focus on the organizational features of paragraphs, essays, or reports. Encourage students to construct a graphic organizer prior to writing and to use the organizer during writing. Recommend that students highlight the components of the written piece (e.g., the topic sentence, supporting details, and concluding sentence in a paragraph) to check for the organizational structure. (Steps 5 and 6)
Voice and Audience Awareness	Guide students to select the voice and style of writing based on the purpose of the writing as identified in the prompt. (Step 6)
Word Choice	Encourage students to select specific vocabulary from the reading material and use strong verbs and adjectives to bring writing to life. Tell them to avoid general words (e.g., *thing*) and the overuse of pronouns. (Steps 3, 5, and 6)
Sentence Fluency	Use the revision process to check for complete sentences and to vary sentence types by combining sentences to form compound and complex sentences. (Steps 4 and 6)
Conventions *Capitalization & Punctuation* *Grammar/Usage* *Spelling*	Use the Handbook section of the *Student Text* for specific skills such as correct use of commas, subject/verb agreement, and application of spelling rules. (Steps 2, 4, and 6)

Baseline Book A: Writing Prompt, Rubric, and Student Responses
Baseline Writing Prompt for Entry into Book A

Prompt:

Think about an item or object (for example, your sneakers, an old sweatshirt, an MP3 player) you own that is so special to you that you cannot do without it. (Do not choose a person or a pet.) Write a paragraph for your classmates in which you describe that object and give reasons why it is so important to you.

Student Instructions:

You will have 45 minutes to complete this assignment. Spend 5-10 minutes organizing your thoughts by making brief notes on a separate sheet of paper. Then write your paragraph in the test booklet, being sure to leave a few minutes to check your work and make any necessary corrections.

You may use a dictionary or a thesaurus to check your word choice and spelling.

Your writing will be scored on how well you:

- Develop a topic sentence for your paragraph that identifies your special item.
- Provide a detailed description of the item and an explanation of why it is so special to you.
- Choose words that are accurate and specific.
- Stay on topic.
- Write complete sentences.
- Apply rules for capitalization, punctuation, grammar/usage, and spelling.

Baseline Writing Rubric for Entry into Book A

Name ______________________ Date ______________________

Grade ______________________ Teacher ______________________

	Criteria				Value	
Trait	**4**	**3**	**2**	**1**		**Teacher Comments**
Ideas and Content	Focuses on the topic. Main idea (topic sentence) is well supported with examples, evidence, and explanations.	Mostly focuses on the topic. Sentences supporting the main idea (topic sentence) may be general rather than detailed and specific.	Main idea (topic sentence) is unclear and/or lacks sufficient support.	Does not address prompt and/or lacks a topic sentence. Supporting details are absent or do not relate to topic.	____	
Organization	Topic sentence clearly states main idea. Ideas logically organized. Contains concluding sentence.	Topic sentence states main idea. Organization mostly logical. May contain concluding sentence.	Structure may not be entirely logical. Paragraph may seem list-like and/or be hard to follow.	No evident structure. Lack of organization seriously interferes with meaning.	____	
Voice and Audience Awareness	Strong sense of person and purpose behind the words. Brings topic to life.	Some sense of person and purpose behind the words.	Little sense of person and purpose behind the words.	No sense of person or purpose behind the words.	____	
Word Choice	Words are specific to the content, accurate, and vivid. Word choice enhances meaning and reader's enjoyment.	Words used correctly but may be somewhat general and unspecific.	Word choice limited. Words may be used inaccurately or repetitively.	Extremely limited range of words. Restricted vocabulary impedes message.	____	
Sentence Fluency	Writes complete sentences, some of which are expanded.	Writes complete sentences.	Writes simple sentences and/or awkwardly structured sentences. May include some run-ons and fragments.	Numerous run-ons and/or fragments interfere with meaning.	____	
Conventions	*Capitalization & Punctuation* 0–1 error. Indents paragraph.	*Capitalization & Punctuation* 2 errors. Indents paragraph.	*Capitalization & Punctuation* 3–5 errors. May not indent paragraph.	*Capitalization & Punctuation* 6+ errors. May not indent paragraph.	____	
	Grammar/Usage 0–1 error	*Grammar/Usage* 2 errors	*Grammar/Usage* 3 errors	*Grammar/Usage* 4+ errors	____	
	Spelling 0–1 error	*Spelling* 2–3 errors	*Spelling* 4–5 errors	*Spelling* 6+ errors	____	

Proficient

Student Response:

The thing I can't live without is ranch dressing! It is smooth and yummy. When I go out to eat I order a sandwich and I ask the watress for ranch dressing. When I order an appitizor, I ask the watress for ranch dressing. When we order pizza, I ask the waitress for ranch dressing. For a snack, I dip chips in ranch dressing. Some people say it is gross, but here is what I say. Don't knock it until you try it!

Commentary:

In this response, the writer addresses all aspects of the assignment. She declares her topic, gives a brief description of ranch dressing ("smooth and yummy"), then recounts the many ways she loves to enjoy it. She has a firm grasp on organization, with a definitive topic sentence, supporting detail sentences, and a conclusion that is a zinger. The writer captures the reader's attention by using repetition as a stylistic device. The response contains a few errors in English language conventions, but they do not interfere with the message.

Writing: Rating Summary

Trait	Score	Comments
Ideas and Content	4	Addresses all aspects of the assignment and develops the topic with several examples.
Organization	4	Topic sentence clearly states main idea. Examples are purposefully ordered (moves from restaurant experience to ordering food in, to snacking at home), and the concluding sentence offers a challenge to the reader.
Voice and Audience Awareness	4	Writer brings topic to life, and her joyful tone engages the reader.
Word Choice	4	Word choice is accurate and vivid.
Sentence Fluency	4	Varies sentence patterns.
Conventions:		There are a few errors in English language conventions, but they do not seriously interfere with meaning.
Capitalization & Punctuation	4	
Grammar/Usage	4	
*Spelling**	3	

*If the same word is misspelled more than once, it counts as one spelling error.

Rating interpretation: This paper received a high proportion of 4's and only one 3, indicating proficiency in the majority of traits.

Developing Proficiency

Student Response:

I can't live without my cell phone, because it is my life. I always call people, write private stuff about me and sometimes text. My phone is made from verizon wireless and it's a pink razr. I got it at costco. It's my first cell phone. I was really excited when I got it. Sometimes my phone feels like my best friend, because I always talk on it. The best part is it has music on it. I think having a phone is fun and you get to use it a lot and talk to friends family and other people.

Commentary:

This response addresses the assignment. The writer describes the phone briefly and offers general statements about how her cell phone "is my life." She structures the paragraph with an adequate topic sentence ("I can't live without my cell phone because it is my life") and an effective conclusion. However, there is no apparent order to the arrangement of the supporting sentences, and "I got it at Costco" is a bit of a bird walk. Though there are several errors in English language conventions, they are not the sorts that impede the author's message.

Writing: Rating Summary

Trait	Score	Comments
Ideas and Content	3	Mostly focused on the topic. Supporting sentences are general but develop the topic.
Organization	2	Has both a topic sentence and a conclusion; no discernible order in the arrangement of supporting sentences.
Voice and Audience Awareness	3	Some sense of person behind the words. There is an inconsistent sense of audience, but the reader feels the writer's excitement at possessing a cell phone.
Word Choice	3	Word choice accurate but somewhat general rather than specific.
Sentence Fluency	3	Writes mostly simple sentences.
Conventions:		Although there are many errors in punctuation, they do not seriously interfere with the author's meaning.
Capitalization & Punctuation	1	
Grammar/Usage	4	
*Spelling**	4	

*If the same word is misspelled more than once, it counts as one spelling error.

Rating interpretation: This paper received a majority of 3's with a few high (4) and one low (1) score, indicating developing proficiency in the majority of traits.

Emerging Proficiency

Student Response:

I am writing about my Playstation2. My Playstation2 is important for me becuase theres alot of games to play. Theres some games that are my favorite. And becuase is the best machine you coud ever have. Becuase is fun and becuase I get to play when ever I want.

Commentary:

The writer addresses the topic but doesn't develop it sufficiently. The topic sentence is unclear, and supporting details are few in number and overly general in character. The writer has favorite games but doesn't name them; playing with the Playstation 2 is "fun." There is no description of the object. A pervasive lack of details results in lack of voice and audience awareness. A number of grammatical and spelling errors impede the reader's progress through the paragraph.

Writing: Rating Summary

Trait	Score	Comments
Ideas and Content	2	Attempts to address topic but not enough details devoted to developing it.
Organization	2	No clear topic sentence. A few general statements instead of details produce a list-like quality.
Voice and Audience Awareness	2	Little sense of audience awareness.
Word Choice	1	Vocabulary extremely limited.
Sentence Fluency	2	Simple sentences. Sentence fragment.
Conventions:		Many grammatical and a few spelling errors obscure the author's meaning.
Capitalization & Punctuation	3	
Grammar/Usage	1	
*Spelling**	3	

*When the same word is misspelled more than once, it counts as one spelling error.

Rating interpretation: This paper received mostly 2 ratings with a few higher (3) or lower (1) scores, indicating emerging proficiency in the majority of traits.

Not Proficient

Student Response:

I Cannot live without an ipod becuase it wouldnt be fair to listen to it when I want to. But I love ipods. Becuase its fair to me and some other people too. Ipods are awesome they are great to listen to allday. It wouldnt be fair. The ipods are small.

Commentary:

The writer attempts to address the topic, but the connection between the ideas in the paragraph is bewildering; the reader cannot grasp the writer's meaning. The writer notes that her MP3 player is "small" but does not otherwise provide specific details describing the object and its functions. Lack of control over organization and the limited vocabulary result in poor audience awareness. There are several errors in conventions of the English language in this short paragraph.

Writing: Rating Summary

Trait	Score	Comments
Ideas and Content	1	Connection between ideas in the paragraph is puzzling. No clear development of topic.
Organization	1	No control over organization. Hard to follow thread of meaning.
Voice and Audience Awareness	1	No sense of audience.
Word Choice	1	Extremely limited vocabulary.
Sentence Fluency	1	Difficulty constructing sentences that convey meaning.
Conventions:		Several errors in the conventions of the English language make the writer's message unclear.
Capitalization & Punctuation	1	
Grammar/Usage	3	
*Spelling**	3	

*If same word is misspelled more than once, it counts as one spelling error.

Rating interpretation: This paper received mostly 1 ratings with two higher (3) ratings, indicating no proficiency in the majority of traits.

Book A: Writing Prompt, Rubric, and Sample Student Responses

Book A Progress Indicator Writing Prompt

Prompt:

Everyone has a favorite type of music (for example, rock, pop, country and western, classical, jazz). What is your favorite type of music? Write a paragraph in which you identify your favorite type of music and explain why you like it so much. Be sure to include supporting details.

Student Instructions:

You will have 45 minutes to complete this assignment. Spend 5–10 minutes organizing your thoughts by making brief notes on a separate sheet of paper. Then write your paragraph, being sure to leave a few minutes to check your work and make any corrections necessary.

You may use a dictionary or a thesaurus to check your word choice and spelling.

Your writing will be scored on how well you:

- Develop a topic sentence for your paragraph that identifies your favorite type of music.
- Provide a detailed explanation of why __________ is your favorite type of music.
- Stay on topic.
- Choose words that engage the reader and are specific to the content.
- Write complete sentences.
- Apply rules for capitalization, punctuation, grammar/usage, and spelling.

Book A Writing Rubric

Name ____________________ Date ____________________

Grade ____________________ Teacher ____________________

	Criteria				Value	
Trait	**4**	**3**	**2**	**1**		**Teacher Comments**
Ideas and Content	Focuses on the topic. Main idea (topic sentence) is well supported with details and elaboration (examples, evidence, and explanations).	Mostly focuses on the topic. Sentences supporting the main idea (topic sentence) may be general rather than detailed and specific.	Main idea (topic sentence) is unclear and/or lacks sufficient support.	Does not address prompt and/or lacks a topic sentence. Supporting details are absent or do not relate to topic.	____	
Organization	Topic sentence clearly states main idea. Ideas are clear and logically organized. Contains concluding sentence.	Topic sentence states main idea. Organization mostly clear and logical. May contain concluding sentence.	Structure may not be entirely clear or logical. Paragraph may seem more like a list and/or be hard to follow.	No evident structure. Lack of organization seriously interferes with meaning.	____	
Voice and Audience Awareness	Strong sense of a person and purpose behind the words. Brings topic to life.	Some sense of person and purpose behind the words.	Little sense of person and purpose behind the words.	No sense of person or purpose behind the words. No sense of audience.	____	
Word Choice	Words are specific to the content, accurate, and vivid. Word choice enhances meaning and reader's enjoyment.	Words are correctly used but may be somewhat general and unspecific.	Words may be used inaccurately or repetitively.	Extremely limited range of words. Restricted vocabulary impedes message.	____	
Sentence Fluency	Writes complete sentences and varies sentence structure.	Writes complete sentences and attempts to use expanded sentences.	Writes mostly simple and/or awkwardly constructed sentences. May include some run-ons and fragments.	Numerous run-ons and/or fragments interfere with meaning.	____	
Conventions	*Capitalization & Punctuation* 0–1 error. Indents paragraph.	*Capitalization & Punctuation* 2 errors. Indents paragraph.	*Capitalization & Punctuation* 3 errors. May not indent paragraph.	*Capitalization & Punctuation* 4+ errors. May not indent paragraph.	____	
	Grammar/Usage 0–1 error	*Grammar/Usage* 2 errors	*Grammar/Usage* 3 errors	*Grammar/Usage* 4+ errors	____	
	Spelling 0–1 error	*Spelling* 2 errors	*Spelling* 3 errors	*Spelling* 4+ errors	____	

Proficient

Student Response:

My favorite type of music is R and B, which is a combination of jazz and the blues. R and B helps me do my homework and the strong beat makes my body want to dance. It is good party music. R and B music can send me to sleep or when I set my alarm clock to an R and B station, it can me wake up fast. These are just some of the reasons that I like R and B music.

Commentary:

In this response, the writer addresses all parts of the writing task. He identifies his favorite type of music (R and B) and uses supporting details to explain why he likes it so much (helps him with homework, helps him go to sleep, etc.) The writer displays a capacity for organization by starting his paragraph with a topic sentence, ending with a simple concluding sentence, and logically arraying his reasons. There is a sense of a person behind the words ("the strong beat makes my body want to dance") that draws the reader to the writer.

Writing: Rating Summary

Trait	Score	Comments
Ideas and Content	4	Writer addresses all parts of the writing task and develops topic with details.
Organization	4	Has topic sentence and concluding sentence. Supporting details logically arranged.
Voice and Audience Awareness	3	Engages the reader with a sense of person behind the words.
Word Choice	3	Words are accurate and specific to content.
Sentence Fluency	4	Some variation in structure.
Conventions:		Minimal errors in the conventions of the English language.
Capitalization & Punctuation	3	
Grammar/Usage	4	
*Spelling**	4	

*If a word is misspelled more than once, it counts as one spelling error.

Rating interpretation: This paper received a high proportion of 4's and a few 3's, indicating proficiency in a majority of traits.

Developing Proficiency

Student Response:

My favorite type of music is hip-hop. Hip-hop lyrics are cool and I can understand the words. I like listening to hip-hop because I can dance to it. Hip-hop is great for extersizeing. For me, hip-hop is the only kind of music I want to listen to.

Commentary:

In this response, the writer addresses all parts of the assignment. He identifies his favorite type of music (hip-hop) and uses supporting details to outline his reasons (good to dance to, good for exercising, etc.). The writer displays some sense of organization, starting the paragraph with a topic sentence and ending it with a concluding sentence. The support for the topic sentence is general and the details skate on the edge of being list-like. The writer's voice is evident in his enthusiasm for hip-hop.

Writing: Rating Summary

Trait	Score	Comments
Ideas and Content	3	Focused on the topic. Supporting sentences offer general statements rather than detailed support.
Organization	3	Has topic sentence and concluding sentence.
Voice and Audience Awareness	3	Sense of enthusiasm about the topic.
Word Choice	3	Words used accurately.
Sentence Fluency	2	Mostly simple sentences.
Conventions:		There are a few errors in the conventions of the English language, but they do not impede the writer's message.
Capitalization & Punctuation	4	
Grammar/Usage	4	
*Spelling**	4	

*If the same word is misspelled twice, it counts as one spelling error.

Rating interpretation: This paper received a majority of 3's with a few higher (4) and one lower (2) rating, indicating developing proficiency in the majority of traits.

Emerging Proficiency

Student Response:

My favorite type of music is hiphop. I like hiphop becuase the beat sound good. Hiphop songs are the best songs that I ever herd befor. Hiphop are good at rap and they have the best beat and music.

Commentary:

In this response, the writer addresses one part of the writing assignment (identifying his favorite type of music), but does not develop the topic sufficiently. He starts with a topic sentence ("My favorite type of music is hiphop") and supports it only with very general and repetitive statements (e.g., "Hiphop songs are the best songs."). The writer wanders instead of creating a purposeful organization for his paragraph, and his lack of detail means that the reader hasn't much sense of the writer's voice.

Writing: Rating Summary

Trait	Score	Comments
Ideas and Content	2	Addresses one part of the assignment, but does not develop topic sufficiently.
Organization	2	Has topic sentence; paragraph is list-like with no purposeful organization.
Voice and Audience Awareness	1	No sense of audience.
Word Choice	1	Extremely limited vocabulary.
Sentence Fluency	2	Awkward structure.
Conventions:		In this short paragraph there are several grammatical and spelling errors.
Capitalization & Punctuation	4	
Grammar/Usage	3	
*Spelling**	1	

*If the same word is misspelled more than once, it counts as one spelling error.

Rating interpretation: This paper received a mix of 2 and 1 ratings with a few higher (3 and 4) ratings, indicating emerging proficiency in the majority of traits.

Not Proficient

Student Response:

The music I like is Hip-Hop. Hip-Hop it rlax you a lot. The learix are so quiet. My favorite type of music is Hip-Hop because it rlax you a lot, I like the lyrilxs that whay like Hip-Hop.

Commentary:

This response begins to address the topic, but fails to develop it. There is a topic sentence ("The music I like is Hip-Hop), but there are only two details (music relaxes you, lyrics are quiet) and they are repeated twice. The lack of organization interferes with meaning. Very limited word choice and extensive sentence and spelling errors constitute a lack of audience awareness.

Writing: Rating Summary

Trait	Score	Comments
Ideas and Content	2	This response begins to address the topic, but fails to develop it.
Organization	1	There is a topic sentence ("The music I like is Hip-Hop), but there are only two details (music relaxes you, lyrics are quiet) and they are repeated twice. The lack of organization interferes with meaning.
Voice and Audience Awareness	1	No sense of audience.
Word Choice	1	Extremely limited word choice fails to engage the reader.
Sentence Fluency	1	Sentence errors interfere with meaning.
Conventions:		Paragraph not indented. Sentence and spelling errors seriously impede the writer's message.
Capitalization & Punctuation	4	
Grammar/Usage	2	
*Spelling**	1	

*If the same word is misspelled more than once, it counts as one spelling error.

Rating interpretation: This paper received mostly 1 ratings, indicating no proficiency in the majority of traits.

Appendix A

- TOSCRF Scoring Exercises

TOSCRF Scoring Exercises

The following 10 exercises are completed examples of Student Record Forms. For each example, use the scoring procedures described in this booklet. See Table A.1 at the end of Appendix A for the correct scores. Do not attempt to score the TOSCRF in an actual testing situation until your scores match the correct scores. You may photocopy the exercises in this appendix for training purposes.

Example A.1—Form A

1. YOUCAN

2. LOOKDOWN

3. JUMPUPRUNFAST

4. SEEFATHERWESING

5. AYELLOWBIRDWITHBLUEWINGSSATONMOTHERSPRETTY HATITWASTHEMISSINGBIRD

6. THEFOXGAVETHESTORKABITOFTHESOUPINASHALLOW DISHBUTTHESTORKCOULDNOTEATFROMTHEDISH

7. THEBOYSWENTINTOASTOREANDLOOKEDATBOOKSABOUT ANIMALSONEBOYSAWABOOKABOUTHORSES

8. THESTORKSERVEDTHESOUPINTWOTALLBOTTLESWITH THINNARROWNECKSSHESTUCKHERLONGBILLINTOTHE BOTTLEANDATEEVERYDROP

9. SOMEDAYSAFTERWARDTHESTORKINVITEDTHEFOXTO DINNERSHEHADMADESOMEDELICIOUSSOUPANDTHEFOX WASVERYHUNGRY

10. ASTHECLOCKTICKEDOFFONEMINUTEAFTERANOTHER EACHOFTHEGIRLSTRIEDTOPINARIBBONONTHELIONS TAILTHEYPUTRIBBONSONTHELIONSPAWSHEADAND BODYWHICHGAVEHIMAFRIENDLYLOOK

11. THISMANWASONEOFTHEFIRSTEUROPEANTRAVELERSTO VISITTHEDISTANTREGIONOFCHINAHELEARNEDSEVERAL LANGUAGESSPOKENTHEREANDSERVEDITSGREATRULERS FORMANYYEARS

12. ASAYOUTHHETRAVELEDFROMONEFARMTOANOTHER PICKINGCROPSASTHEYRIPENEDSINCEHISFAMILYHAD NOPERMANENTHOMEHEHADATTENDEDAMULTITUDE OFDIFFERENTSCHOOLSBYTHETIMEHEREACHED THESEVENTHGRADE

Scoring

Raw Score ______

Grade Equiv. ______

Appendix A

Example A.2—Form D

1. IRIDE

2. COMENOW

3. GOHERELOOKUP

4. FINDHIMSTAYHERE

5. ITWASTHEDAYFORTHESCHOOLPICNICALLTHEFOODWAS ONATABLEUNDERATREE

6. WHENTHECHILDRENWEREREADYTHEYHELPEDTHEIR FATHERLOOKFORTHECARKEYSMOTHERKISSEDTHEM ALLANDSAIDHAVEANICEDAY

7. ONEDAYSOMECHILDRENWEREPLAYINGINTHESNOWTHEY WEREMAKINGSNOWANIMALS

8. ITWASPETDAYATTHESTATEFAIRUNDERTHEBIGPINK TENTTHECHILDRENWEREWAITINGFORTHEPARADEOF ANIMALSTOBEGIN

9. ITISDIFFICULTFORANYTHINGTOLIVEINADESERTMANY DESERTANIMALSSPENDMUCHOFTHEIRTIMESEARCHING FORWATERHOLES

10. ANELEPHANTWASWALKINGTHROUGHTHEJUNGLEALONE FRIGHTENEDTHATHEMIGHTCOMEUPONASNAKEHEHAD NEVERSEENASNAKEBEFOREBUTHEHADHEARDWHAT TERRIBLECREATURESTHEYWERE

11. SHELEDGROUPSOFSLAVESFROMONEPOINTTOANOTHER ONTHEPERILOUSJOURNEYNORTHTHEYTRAVELEDONLY AFTERNIGHTFALLHIDINGDURINGTHEDAYINBASEMENTS FIELDSANDFORESTS

12. CIVILIANAIRPLANEPILOTSHAVEMANYIMPORTANTJOBS THEYTRANSPORTPASSENGERSFREIGHTANDMAILFROM ONECITYTOANOTHER

Scoring

Raw Score ______

Grade Equiv. ______

Example A.3—Form D

1. IRIDE

2. COMENOW

3. GOHERELOOKUP

4. FINDHIMSTAYHERE

5. ITWASTHEDAYFORTHESCHOOLPICNICALLTHEFOODWAS ONATABLEUNDERATREE

6. WHENTHECHILDRENWEREREADYTHEYHELPEDTHEIR FATHERLOOKFORTHECARKEYSMOTHERKISSEDTHEM ALLANDSAIDHAVEANICEDAY

7. ONEDAYSOMECHILDRENWEREPLAYINGINTHESNOWTHEY WEREMAKINGSNOWANIMALS

8. ITWASPETDAYATTHESTATEFAIRUNDERTHEBIGPINK TENTTHECHILDRENWEREWAITINGFORTHEPARADEOF ANIMALSTOBEGIN

9. ITISDIFFICULTFORANYTHINGTOLIVEINADESERTMANY DESERTANIMALSSPENDMUCHOFTHEIRTIMESEARCHING FORWATERHOLES

10. ANELEPHANTWASWALKINGTHROUGHTHEJUNGLEALONE FRIGHTENEDTHATHEMIGHTCOMEUPONASNAKEHEHAD NEVERSEENASNAKEBEFOREBUTHEHADHEARDWHAT TERRIBLECREATURESTHEYWERE

11. SHELEDGROUPSOFSLAVESFROMONEPOINTTOANOTHER ONTHEPERILOUSJOURNEYNORTHTHEYTRAVELEDONLY AFTERNIGHTFALLHIDINGDURINGTHEDAYINBASEMENTS FIELDSANDFORESTS

12. CIVILIANAIRPLANEPILOTSHAVEMANYIMPORTANTJOBS THEYTRANSPORTPASSENGERSFREIGHTANDMAILFROM ONECITYTOANOTHER

Scoring

Raw Score ______

Grade Equiv. ______

Example A.4—Form C

1. ISEE

2. WERUN

3. COMEHEREDOTHIS

4. HURRYHOMEWALKFAST

5. TWOBOYSRODETHEBUSTOTOWNFIRSTTHEYWALKEDALONG
THESTREETANDLOOKEDATTHINGSINTHESHOPWINDOWS

6. AGIRLRANOUTOFTHEWHITEHOUSEINTOTHEBACKYARD
MOTHERSHESAIDMYLITTLEPETBIRDISGONE

7. TWELVEGIRLSWEREPLAYINGAGAMEATAPARTYONTHEWALL
BEFORETHEMHUNGAPICTUREOFALIONWITHAFIERCE
LOOKINHISEYE

8. THECHILDRENHADTRAINEDTHEIRPETSTODOMANY
DIFFERENTTRICKSINFRONTOFTHEJUDGESONEGIRL
HADABUNNYTHATCOULDCLIMBALADDER

9. AGREEDYFOXWASEATINGALARGEBOWLOFSOUPWHEN
ASTORKCAMETOCALLDISAPPOINTEDATHAVINGTOSHARE
HISSUPPERTHEFOXGAVETHESTORKABITOFTHESOUP
INASHALLOWDISH

10. THELONGTRAILDRIVESTOTHENORTHINWHICHTHE
COWBOYSSKILLATHERDINGCATTLEWASESSENTIAL
BECAMEATHINGOFTHEPASTWITHTHECOMINGOFTHE
RAILROADCATTLECOULDBESHIPPEDDIRECTLYTOMARKET

11. THEAPPLAUDINGSPECTATORSFELLSILENTTHEYHAD
CHEEREDTHEDAUNTLESSWARRIORSTHROUGHEIGHT
BRUTALINNINGSAGAINSTTHEIRFIERCESTRIVALS

12. MUCHOFOURUNDERSTANDINGABOUTSHARKSCOMES
FROMTHEDISCOVERIESOFONEENTERPRISINGWOMAN
SHEISASCIENTISTWHOSTUDIESTHEBEHAVIOROFSHARKS

Scoring

Raw Score ______

Grade Equiv. _____

Example A.5—Form A

1. YOUCAN

2. LOOKDOWN

3. JUMPUPRUNFAST

4. SEEFATHERWESING

5. AYELLOWBIRDWITHBLUEWINGSSATONMOTHERSPRETTY HATITWASTHEMISSINGBIRD

6. THEFOXGAVETHESTORKABITOFTHESOUPINASHALLOW DISHBUTTHESTORKCOULDNOTEATFROMTHEDISH

7. THEBOYSWENTINTOASTOREANDLOOKEDATBOOKSABOUT ANIMALSONEBOYSAWABOOKABOUTHORSES

8. THESTORKSERVEDTHESOUPINTWOTALLBOTTLESWITH THINNARROWNECKSSHESTUCKHERLONGBILLINTOTHE BOTTLEANDATEEVERYDROP

9. SOMEDAYSAFTERWARDTHESTORKINVITEDTHEFOXTO DINNERSHEHADMADESOMEDELICIOUSSOUPANDTHEFOX WASVERYHUNGRY

10. ASTHECLOCKTICKEDOFFONEMINUTEAFTERANOTHER EACHOFTHEGIRLSTRIEDTOPINARIBBONONTHELIONS TAILTHEYPUTRIBBONSONTHELIONSPAWSHEADAND BODYWHICHGAVEHIMAFRIENDLYLOOK

11. THISMANWASONEOFTHEFIRSTEUROPEANTRAVELERSTO VISITTHEDISTANTREGIONOFCHINAHELEARNEDSEVERAL LANGUAGESSPOKENTHEREANDSERVEDITSGREATRULERS FORMANYYEARS

12. ASAYOUTHHETRAVELEDFROMONEFARMTOANOTHER PICKINGCROPSASTHEYRIPENEDSINCEHISFAMILYHAD NOPERMANENTHOMEHEHADATTENDEDAMULTITUDE OFDIFFERENTSCHOOLSBYTHETIMEHEREACHED THESEVENTHGRADE

Scoring

Raw Score ________

Grade Equiv. ______

Example A.6—Form C

1. I|SEE
2. WE|RUN
3. COME|HERE|DO|THIS
4. HURRY|HOME|WALK|FAST

Scoring

Raw Score ______

Grade Equiv. ______

Example A.7—Form B

1. GOHOME

2. STOPNOW

3. HELPMERIDEFAST

4. SITDOWNLOOKAROUND

5. TWOGIRLSWENTTOAFARMFORAVISITTHEREWERECOWS PIGSDUCKSANDFIVEHENSTHEGIRLSGATHEREDTHE EGGSEVERYMORNING

6. FATHERWENTOUTTOBUYSOMEPRETTYFLOWERSTHECAKE COOKEDALITTLETOOLONGSOITWASBROWN

7. JUSTASTHECHILDRENWEREREADYTORUNTHERAINBEGAN TOFALLTHETEACHERSAIDHURRYINCHILDREN

8. ONCETHEREWASATURTLEWHOCHATTEREDSOMUCHTHAT SHEHADNOFRIENDSONEDAYSHEMETANEAGLETRAVELING TODISTANTLANDSACROSSTHESEA

9. ONEBRIGHTSUMMERDAYAYOUNGBOYANDHISGRANDMOTHER WALKEDTOANEARBYPONDTOFISHTHEBOYSGRANDMOTHER SHOWEDHIMHOWTOPUTWORMSONTHEHOOKSOTHEYWOULD NOTCOMEOFF

10. FARMERSATTEMPTTOCONTROLPESTSBYUSINGCHEMICALS BUTTHEYCANMAKEOURFOODUNSAFETOEATATANYSEASON OFTHEYEARWEATHERMAYALSODESTROYCROPS

11. DURINGTHEFILMINGOFAMOVIESTARSHAVEANEXHAUSTING SCHEDULETHEIRDAYOFTENBEGINSBEFOREDAWNWITH MAKEUPSESSIONSCOSTUMEFITTINGSORSPECIALTRAINING WITHASPEECHCOACH

12. ALLOVERTHEWORLDFARMERSFACEDIFFICULTPROBLEMS FRUITSVEGETABLESANDOTHERPLANTSAREFREQUENTLY ATTACKEDBYHARMFULINSECTSANDDISEASESTHATCAN WIPEOUTANENTIRECROP

Scoring

Raw Score ________

Grade Equiv. ________

Example A.8—Form B

1. GOHOME

2. STOPNOW

3. HELPMERIDEFAST

4. SITDOWNLOOKAROUND

5. TWOGIRLSWENTTOAFARMFORAVISITTHEREWERECOWS PIGSDUCKSANDFIVEHENSTHEGIRLSGATHEREDTHE EGGSEVERYMORNING

6. FATHERWENTOUTTOBUYSOMEPRETTYFLOWERSTHECAKE COOKEDALITTLETOOLONGSOITWASBROWN

7. JUSTASTHECHILDRENWEREREADYTORUNTHERAINBEGAN TOFALLTHETEACHERSAIDHURRYINCHILDREN

8. ONCETHEREWASATURTLEWHOCHATTEREDSOMUCHTHAT SHEHADNOFRIENDSONEDAYSHEMETANEAGLETRAVELING TODISTANTLANDSACROSSTHESEA

9. ONEBRIGHTSUMMERDAYAYOUNGBOYANDHISGRANDMOTHER WALKEDTOANEARBYPONDTOFISHTHEBOYSGRANDMOTHER SHOWEDHIMHOWTOPUTWORMSONTHEHOOKSOTHEYWOULD NOTCOMEOFF

10. FARMERSATTEMPTTOCONTROLPESTSBYUSINGCHEMICALS BUTTHEYCANMAKEOURFOODUNSAFETOEATATANYSEASON OFTHEYEARWEATHERMAYALSODESTROYCROPS

11. DURINGTHEFILMINGOFAMOVIESTARSHAVEANEXHAUSTING SCHEDULETHEIRDAYOFTENBEGINSBEFOREDAWNWITH MAKEUPSESSIONSCOSTUMEFITTINGSORSPECIALTRAINING WITHASPEECHCOACH

12. ALLOVERTHEWORLDFARMERSFACEDIFFICULTPROBLEMS FRUITSVEGETABLESANDOTHERPLANTSAREFREQUENTLY ATTACKEDBYHARMFULINSECTSANDDISEASESTHATCAN WIPEOUTANENTIRECROP

Scoring

Raw Score ________

Grade Equiv. ______

Example A.9—Form D

1. IRIDE
2. COMENOW
3. GOHERELOOKUP
4. FINDHIMSTAYHERE
5. ITWASTHEDAYFORTHESCHOOLPICNICALLTHEFOODWAS ONATABLEUNDERATREE
6. WHENTHECHILDRENWEREREADYTHEYHELPEDTHEIR FATHERLOOKFORTHECARKEYSMOTHERKISSEDTHEM ALLANDSAIDHAVEANICEDAY
7. ONEDAYSOMECHILDRENWEREPLAYINGINTHESNOWTHEY WEREMAKINGSNOWANIMALS
8. ITWASPETDAYATTHESTATEFAIRUNDERTHEBIGPINK TENTTHECHILDRENWEREWAITINGFORTHEPARADEOF ANIMALSTOBEGIN
9. ITISDIFFICULTFORANYTHINGTOLIVEINADESERTMANY DESERTANIMALSSPENDMUCHOFTHEIRTIMESEARCHING FORWATERHOLES
10. ANELEPHANTWASWALKINGTHROUGHTHEJUNGLEALONE FRIGHTENEDTHATHEMIGHTCOMEUPONASNAKEHEHAD NEVERSEENASNAKEBEFOREBUTHEHADHEARDWHAT TERRIBLECREATURESTHEYWERE
11. SHELEDGROUPSOFSLAVESFROMONEPOINTTOANOTHER ONTHEPERILOUSJOURNEYNORTHTHEYTRAVELEDONLY AFTERNIGHTFALLHIDINGDURINGTHEDAYINBASEMENTS FIELDSANDFORESTS
12. CIVILIANAIRPLANEPILOTSHAVEMANYIMPORTANTJOBS THEYTRANSPORTPASSENGERSFREIGHTANDMAILFROM ONECITYTOANOTHER

Scoring

Raw Score ________

Grade Equiv. ______

Appendix A

Example A.10—Form A

1. YOUCAN

2. LOOKDOWN

3. JUMPUPRUNFAST

4. SEEFATHERWESING

5. AYELLOWBIRDWITHBLUEWINGSSATONMOTHERSPRETTY HATITWASTHEMISSINGBIRD

6. THEFOXGAVETHESTORKABITOFTHESOUPINASHALLOW DISHBUTTHESTORKCOULDNOTEATFROMTHEDISH

7. THEBOYSWENTINTOASTOREANDLOOKEDATBOOKSABOUT ANIMALSONEBOYSAWABOOKABOUTHORSES

8. THESTORKSERVEDTHESOUPINTWOTALLBOTTLESWITH THINNARROWNECKSSHESTUCKHERLONGBILLINTOTHE BOTTLEANDATEEVERYDROP

9. SOMEDAYSAFTERWARDTHESTORKINVITEDTHEFOXTO DINNERSHEHADMADESOMEDELICIOUSSOUPANDTHEFOX WASVERYHUNGRY

10. ASTHECLOCKTICKEDOFFONEMINUTEAFTERANOTHER EACHOFTHEGIRLSTRIEDTOPINARIBBONONTHELIONS TAILTHEYPUTRIBBONSONTHELIONSPAWSHEADAND BODYWHICHGAVEHIMAFRIENDLYLOOK

11. THISMANWASONEOFTHEFIRSTEUROPEANTRAVELERSTO VISITTHEDISTANTREGIONOFCHINAHELEARNEDSEVERAL LANGUAGESSPOKENTHEREANDSERVEDITSGREATRULERS FORMANYYEARS

12. ASAYOUTHHETRAVELEDFROMONEFARMTOANOTHER PICKINGCROPSASTHEYRIPENEDSINCEHISFAMILYHAD NOPERMANENTHOMEHEHADATTENDEDAMULTITUDE OFDIFFERENTSCHOOLSBYTHETIMEHEREACHED THESEVENTHGRADE

Scoring

Raw Score ______

Grade Equiv. ______

Table A.1: Key for Scoring Examples			
Student		TOSCRF Values	
Example	Form	Raw Score	Grade Equivalent
A.1	A	58	3.0
A.2	D	122	7.2
A.3	D	88	4.4
A.4	C	114	7.0
A.5	A	137	10.4
A.6	C	158	12.7
A.7	B	0*	
A.8	B	132	10.0
A.9	D	173	>13.0
A.10	A	201	>13.0

*Could not score because of skipped lines.

For Scoring Exercises Only

Form A

		Line Word Count	Total Word Count
1.	YOU CAN	2	2
2.	LOOK DOWN	2	4
3.	JUMP UP RUN FAST	4	8
4.	SEE FATHER WE SING	4	12
5.	A YELLOW BIRD WITH BLUE WINGS SAT ON MOTHERS PRETTY	10	22
	HAT IT WAS THE MISSING BIRD	6	28
6.	THE FOX GAVE THE STORK A BIT OF THE SOUP IN A SHALLOW	13	41
	DISH BUT THE STORK COULD NOT EAT FROM THE DISH	10	51
7.	THE BOYS WENT INTO A STORE AND LOOKED AT BOOKS ABOUT	11	62
	ANIMALS ONE BOY SAW A BOOK ABOUT HORSES	8	70
8.	THE STORK SERVED THE SOUP IN TWO TALL BOTTLES WITH	10	80
	THIN NARROW NECKS SHE STUCK HER LONG BILL INTO THE	10	90
	BOTTLE AND ATE EVERY DROP	5	95
9.	SOME DAYS AFTERWARD THE STORK INVITED THE FOX TO	9	104
	DINNER SHE HAD MADE SOME DELICIOUS SOUP AND THE FOX	10	114
	WAS VERY HUNGRY	3	117
10.	AS THE CLOCK TICKED OFF ONE MINUTE AFTER ANOTHER	9	126
	EACH OF THE GIRLS TRIED TO PIN A RIBBON ON THE LIONS	12	138
	TAIL THEY PUT RIBBONS ON THE LIONS PAWS HEAD AND	10	148
	BODY WHICH GAVE HIM A FRIENDLY LOOK	7	155
11.	THIS MAN WAS ONE OF THE FIRST EUROPEAN TRAVELERS TO	10	165
	VISIT THE DISTANT REGION OF CHINA HE LEARNED SEVERAL	9	174
	LANGUAGES SPOKEN THERE AND SERVED ITS GREAT RULERS	8	182
	FOR MANY YEARS	3	185

<table>
<tr><th></th><th></th><th>Line Word Count</th><th>Total Word Count</th></tr>
<tr><td>12.</td><td>AS|A|YOUTH|HE|TRAVELED|FROM|ONE|FARM|TO|ANOTHER</td><td>10</td><td>195</td></tr>
<tr><td></td><td>PICKING|CROPS|AS|THEY|RIPENED|SINCE|HIS|FAMILY|HAD</td><td>9</td><td>204</td></tr>
<tr><td></td><td>NO|PERMANENT|HOME|HE|HAD|ATTENDED|A|MULTITUDE</td><td>8</td><td>212</td></tr>
<tr><td></td><td>OF|DIFFERENT|SCHOOLS|BY|THE|TIME|HE|REACHED</td><td>8</td><td>220</td></tr>
<tr><td></td><td>THE|SEVENTH|GRADE</td><td>3</td><td>223</td></tr>
<tr><td>13.</td><td>THE|YOUNG|MAN|WAS|DELIGHTED|TO|OBTAIN|HIS|DEPUTY</td><td>9</td><td>232</td></tr>
<tr><td></td><td>SHERIFFS|BADGE|AS|HIS|FIRST|ASSIGNMENT|HE|HAD|BEEN</td><td>9</td><td>241</td></tr>
<tr><td></td><td>APPOINTED|TO|ESCORT|A|PRISONER|TO|THE|AUTHORITIES|AT</td><td>9</td><td>250</td></tr>
<tr><td></td><td>THE|COUNTY|SEAT|AND|THE|SITE|OF|THE|IMPENDING|TRIAL</td><td>10</td><td>260</td></tr>
<tr><td>14.</td><td>THERE|ARE|SUNDRY|DEFINITIONS|OF|JAZZ|ALL|OF|THEM|VAGUE</td><td>10</td><td>270</td></tr>
<tr><td></td><td>THEIR|VAGUENESS|SEEMS|IMPERATIVE|HOWEVER|IF|THEY</td><td>7</td><td>277</td></tr>
<tr><td></td><td>ARE|TO|ACCOMMODATE|THE|CUSTOM|OF|JAZZ|TO|APPROPRIATE</td><td>9</td><td>286</td></tr>
<tr><td></td><td>EVERYTHING|IN|SIGHT</td><td>3</td><td>289</td></tr>
<tr><td>15.</td><td>AS|THE|EMPERORS|AGENT|HE|EXPLORED|THE|FAR|CORNERS</td><td>9</td><td>298</td></tr>
<tr><td></td><td>OF|THE|KINGDOM|HE|KEPT|A|NOTEBOOK|FILLED|WITH</td><td>9</td><td>307</td></tr>
<tr><td></td><td>FASCINATING|ACCOUNTS|OF|HIS|EXPERIENCES|AS|WELL|AS</td><td>8</td><td>315</td></tr>
<tr><td></td><td>ECONOMIC|AND|POLITICAL|REPORTS|FOR|THE|EMPERORS|USE</td><td>8</td><td>323</td></tr>
<tr><td>16.</td><td>THE|ADROIT|MAN|WAS|AFFABLE|IN|DEBATE|AND|OF|THAT</td><td>10</td><td>333</td></tr>
<tr><td></td><td>SEEMING|HUMILITY|AND|SUBMISSION|OF|JUDGMENT|AS|IF|HE</td><td>9</td><td>342</td></tr>
<tr><td></td><td>BROUGHT|NO|OPINIONS|WITH|HIM|BUT|RATHER|A|FIDELITY|TO</td><td>10</td><td>352</td></tr>
<tr><td></td><td>ENLIGHTENMENT|AND|INSTRUCTION|HE|HAD|SO|SUBTLE</td><td>7</td><td>359</td></tr>
<tr><td></td><td>A|WAY|OF|INTERROGATING|THE|OTHER|MINISTERS|AND|UNDER</td><td>9</td><td>368</td></tr>
<tr><td></td><td>THE|GUISE|OF|SKEPTICISM|INSINUATING|HIS|OBJECTIONS</td><td>7</td><td>375</td></tr>
<tr><td></td><td>TO|A|PROPOSED|EDICT|THAT|HE|INSTILLED|HIS|PERSPECTIVE</td><td>9</td><td>384</td></tr>
<tr><td></td><td>IN|THOSE|FROM|WHOM|HE|PRETENDED|TO|LEARN</td><td>8</td><td>392</td></tr>
<tr><td>17.</td><td>CERTAINLY|SHE|HAD|LATELY|BEEN|COGNIZANT|OF|THE|SUAVE</td><td>9</td><td>401</td></tr>
<tr><td></td><td>YOUNG|MANS|UNNECESSARY|CHIVALRY|BUT|SHE|HAD</td><td>7</td><td>408</td></tr>
<tr><td></td><td>CONSTRUED|IT|WAS|AN|ABERRATION|OF|JUDGMENT|OR|TASTE</td><td>9</td><td>417</td></tr>
<tr><td></td><td>AS|ONE|PROOF|AMONG|OTHERS|THAT|HE|HAD|NOT|ALWAYS</td><td>10</td><td>427</td></tr>
<tr><td></td><td>MOVED|IN|THE|BEST|CIRCLES|THAT|WITH|ALL|HIS|ASSIDUOUS</td><td>10</td><td>437</td></tr>
<tr><td></td><td>CONCERN|FOR|HER|THE|ACCOUTREMENTS|OF|TRUE</td><td>7</td><td>444</td></tr>
<tr><td></td><td>GENTILITY|WERE|WANTING|BUT|UNTIL|NOW|SHE|HAD|NEVER</td><td>9</td><td>453</td></tr>
<tr><td></td><td>SURMISED|IT|TO|MEAN|ANYTHING|HIS|MANNER|MUST|HAVE</td><td>9</td><td>462</td></tr>
<tr><td></td><td>BEEN|EQUIVOCAL|OR|SHE|COULD|NOT|HAVE|BEEN|SO|BEGUILED</td><td>10</td><td>472</td></tr>
</table>

For Scoring Exercises Only

Form B

		Line Word Count	Total Word Count
1.	GO HOME	2	2
2.	STOP NOW	2	4
3.	HELP ME RIDE FAST	4	8
4.	SIT DOWN LOOK AROUND	4	12
5.	TWO GIRLS WENT TO A FARM FOR A VISIT THERE WERE COWS	12	24
	PIGS DUCKS AND FIVE HENS THE GIRLS GATHERED THE	9	33
	EGGS EVERY MORNING	3	36
6.	FATHER WENT OUT TO BUY SOME PRETTY FLOWERS THE CAKE	10	46
	COOKED A LITTLE TOO LONG SO IT WAS BROWN	9	55
7.	JUST AS THE CHILDREN WERE READY TO RUN THE RAIN BEGAN	11	66
	TO FALL THE TEACHER SAID HURRY IN CHILDREN	8	74
8.	ONCE THERE WAS A TURTLE WHO CHATTERED SO MUCH THAT	10	84
	SHE HAD NO FRIENDS ONE DAY SHE MET AN EAGLE TRAVELING	11	95
	TO DISTANT LANDS ACROSS THE SEA	6	101
9.	ONE BRIGHT SUMMER DAY A YOUNG BOY AND HIS GRANDMOTHER	10	111
	WALKED TO A NEARBY POND TO FISH THE BOYS GRANDMOTHER	10	121
	SHOWED HIM HOW TO PUT WORMS ON THE HOOKS SO THEY WOULD	12	133
	NOT COME OFF	3	136
10.	FARMERS ATTEMPT TO CONTROL PESTS BY USING CHEMICALS	8	144
	BUT THEY CAN MAKE OUR FOOD UNSAFE TO EAT AT ANY SEASON	12	156
	OF THE YEAR WEATHER MAY ALSO DESTROY CROPS	8	164
11.	DURING THE FILMING OF A MOVIE STARS HAVE AN EXHAUSTING	10	174
	SCHEDULE THEIR DAY OFTEN BEGINS BEFORE DAWN WITH	8	182
	MAKEUP SESSIONS COSTUME FITTINGS OR SPECIAL TRAINING	7	189
	WITH A SPEECH COACH	4	193

<table>
<tr><th></th><th></th><th>Line Word Count</th><th>Total Word Count</th></tr>
<tr><td>12.</td><td>ALL|OVER|THE|WORLD|FARMERS|FACE|DIFFICULT|PROBLEMS</td><td>8</td><td>201</td></tr>
<tr><td></td><td>FRUIT|VEGETABLES|AND|OTHER|PLANTS|ARE|FREQUENTLY</td><td>7</td><td>208</td></tr>
<tr><td></td><td>ATTACKED|BY|HARMFUL|INSECTS|AND|DISEASES|THAT|CAN</td><td>8</td><td>216</td></tr>
<tr><td></td><td>WIPE|OUT|AN|ENTIRE|CROP</td><td>5</td><td>221</td></tr>
<tr><td>13.</td><td>THE|PARK|RANGERS|SOLITARY|VIGIL|WAS|TERMINATED|BY</td><td>8</td><td>229</td></tr>
<tr><td></td><td>THE|STIR|OF|HOOVES|IN|THE|SCRUB|THROUGH|THE|EARLY</td><td>10</td><td>239</td></tr>
<tr><td></td><td>DIMNESS|SHE|COULD|PERCEIVE|THE|FLUID|CONTOURS|OF</td><td>8</td><td>247</td></tr>
<tr><td></td><td>THE|MAJESTIC|CREATURES|AS|THEY|ASSEMBLED|AT</td><td>7</td><td>254</td></tr>
<tr><td></td><td>THE|ARTESIAN|SPRING</td><td>3</td><td>257</td></tr>
<tr><td>14.</td><td>THE|GALES|FURY|BEGAN|TO|INTENSIFY|AS|THE|STEADFAST</td><td>9</td><td>266</td></tr>
<tr><td></td><td>GIRL|LUGGED|THE|SPLINTERED|ROWBOAT|ONTO|THE|BARREN</td><td>8</td><td>274</td></tr>
<tr><td></td><td>REEF|HER|YOUNGER|BROTHER|HAD|MANAGED|TO|STUMBLE</td><td>8</td><td>282</td></tr>
<tr><td></td><td>TO|SHORE|THROUGH|THE|CHURNING|SURF|DESPITE|THE|GASH</td><td>9</td><td>291</td></tr>
<tr><td></td><td>ON|HIS|LEG|AND|POSSIBLY|A|FRACTURED|WRIST</td><td>8</td><td>299</td></tr>
<tr><td>15.</td><td>THIS|FAMOUS|AMERICAN|WOMAN|BECAME|THE|LEADER|OF</td><td>8</td><td>307</td></tr>
<tr><td></td><td>THE|UNDERGROUND|RAILROAD|A|SECRET|NETWORK|OF</td><td>7</td><td>317</td></tr>
<tr><td></td><td>HOUSEHOLDS|THAT|PROVIDED|FOOD|AND|SHELTER|TO</td><td>7</td><td>321</td></tr>
<tr><td></td><td>RUNAWAY|SLAVES|SHE|LED|GROUPS|OF|SLAVES|FROM|ONE</td><td>9</td><td>330</td></tr>
<tr><td></td><td>POINT|TO|ANOTHER|ON|THE|PERILOUS|JOURNEY|NORTH</td><td>8</td><td>338</td></tr>
<tr><td>16.</td><td>A|LEGEND|IS|A|TRADITIONAL|ORAL|NARRATIVE|REGARDED</td><td>8</td><td>346</td></tr>
<tr><td></td><td>AS|TRUE|BY|ITS|TELLER|AND|THE|SOCIETY|IN|WHICH|IT</td><td>11</td><td>357</td></tr>
<tr><td></td><td>CIRCULATES|LIKE|OTHER|CATEGORIES|OF|FOLKLORE</td><td>6</td><td>363</td></tr>
<tr><td></td><td>LEGENDS|FREQUENTLY|BECOME|EMBELLISHED|WITH</td><td>5</td><td>368</td></tr>
<tr><td></td><td>EXAGGERATED|OR|SUPERNATURAL|ELEMENTS|THAT|MAKE</td><td>6</td><td>374</td></tr>
<tr><td></td><td>THEM|HIGHLY|IMPLAUSIBLE</td><td>3</td><td>377</td></tr>
<tr><td>17.</td><td>THE|QUEEN|WAS|ONE|OF|THE|POTENTATES|WHO|ATTEMPTED</td><td>9</td><td>386</td></tr>
<tr><td></td><td>THINGS|THAT|NO|REPUTABLE|SOVEREIGN|WOULD|HAVE</td><td>7</td><td>393</td></tr>
<tr><td></td><td>DARED|VENTURE|ON|AND|ACHIEVED|THOSE|IN|WHICH|NONE</td><td>9</td><td>402</td></tr>
<tr><td></td><td>BUT|THE|MOST|INTREPID|COULD|HAVE|SUCCEEDED|SHE</td><td>8</td><td>410</td></tr>
<tr><td></td><td>CONSULTED|WITH|VERY|FEW|UPON|ANY|ACTION|OF|IMPORT</td><td>9</td><td>419</td></tr>
<tr><td></td><td>NOR|CONVEYED|ANY|ENTERPRISE|WITH|MORE|THAN|THOSE</td><td>8</td><td>427</td></tr>
<tr><td></td><td>WHO|WERE|TO|HAVE|PRINCIPAL|PARTS|IN|THE|EXECUTION</td><td>9</td><td>436</td></tr>
<tr><td></td><td>OF|IT|NO|SOONER|THAN|WAS|ABSOLUTELY|NECESSARY</td><td>8</td><td>444</td></tr>
</table>

For Scoring Exercises Only

Form C

		Line Word Count	Total Word Count
1.	I SEE	2	2
2.	WE RUN	2	4
3.	COME HERE DO THIS	4	8
4.	HURRY HOME WALK FAST	4	12
5.	TWO BOYS RODE THE BUS TO TOWN FIRST THEY WALKED ALONG	11	23
	THE STREET AND LOOKED AT THINGS IN THE SHOP WINDOWS	10	33
6.	A GIRL RAN OUT OF THE WHITE HOUSE INTO THE BACKYARD	11	44
	MOTHER SHE SAID MY LITTLE PET BIRD IS GONE	9	53
7.	TWELVE GIRLS WERE PLAYING A GAME AT A PARTY ON THE WALL	12	65
	BEFORE THEM HUNG A PICTURE OF A LION WITH A FIERCE	11	76
	LOOK IN HIS EYE	4	80
8.	THE CHILDREN HAD TRAINED THEIR PETS TO DO MANY	9	89
	DIFFERENT TRICKS IN FRONT OF THE JUDGES ONE GIRL	9	98
	HAD A BUNNY THAT COULD CLIMB A LADDER	8	106
9.	A GREEDY FOX WAS EATING A LARGE BOWL OF SOUP WHEN	11	117
	A STORK CAME TO CALL DISAPPOINTED AT HAVING TO SHARE	10	127
	HIS SUPPER THE FOX GAVE THE STORK A BIT OF THE SOUP	12	139
	IN A SHALLOW DISH	4	143
10.	THE LONG TRAIL DRIVES TO THE NORTH IN WHICH THE	10	153
	COWBOYS SKILL AT HERDING CATTLE WAS ESSENTIAL	7	160
	BECAME A THING OF THE PAST WITH THE COMING OF THE	11	171
	RAILROAD CATTLE COULD BE SHIPPED DIRECTLY TO MARKET	8	179
11.	THE APPLAUDING SPECTATORS FELL SILENT THEY HAD	7	186
	CHEERED THE DAUNTLESS WARRIORS THROUGH EIGHT	6	192
	BRUTAL INNINGS AGAINST THEIR FIERCEST RIVALS	6	198

<table>
<tr><th></th><th></th><th>Line Word Count</th><th>Total Word Count</th></tr>
<tr><td>12.</td><td>MUCH|OF|OUR|UNDERSTANDING|ABOUT|SHARKS|COMES</td><td>7</td><td>205</td></tr>
<tr><td></td><td>FROM|THE|DISCOVERIES|OF|ONE|ENTERPRISING|WOMAN</td><td>7</td><td>212</td></tr>
<tr><td></td><td>SHE|IS|A|SCIENTIST|WHO|STUDIES|THE|BEHAVIOR|OF|SHARKS</td><td>10</td><td>222</td></tr>
<tr><td>13.</td><td>THE|EXPANSION|OF|THE|SCHOOL|BUILDING|STOOD|IN</td><td>8</td><td>230</td></tr>
<tr><td></td><td>BOLD|CONTRAST|TO|THE|PLEBEIAN|HALLS|AND|DOORWAYS</td><td>8</td><td>238</td></tr>
<tr><td></td><td>OF|THE|OLD|STRUCTURE|CROSSING|THE|THRESHOLD|FROM</td><td>8</td><td>246</td></tr>
<tr><td></td><td>THE|DRAB|EDIFICE|BUILT|DURING|THE|DEPRESSION|ONE</td><td>8</td><td>254</td></tr>
<tr><td></td><td>WAS|THRUST|INTO|A|SWIRLING|WEB|OF|CURVED|LINES</td><td>9</td><td>263</td></tr>
<tr><td></td><td>RECESSED|LIGHTS|AND|BRIGHT|COLORS</td><td>5</td><td>268</td></tr>
<tr><td>14.</td><td>IN|THE|THIRTEENTH|CENTURY|THE|PEOPLE|OF|EUROPE|WERE</td><td>9</td><td>277</td></tr>
<tr><td></td><td>IGNORANT|ABOUT|MANY|REMOTE|AREAS|OF|THE|WORLD</td><td>8</td><td>285</td></tr>
<tr><td></td><td>CHINA|A|VAST|AND|POWERFUL|COUNTRY|IN|ASIA|WAS</td><td>9</td><td>294</td></tr>
<tr><td></td><td>UNCHARTED|TERRITORY|ON|THE|EUROPEANS|MAP</td><td>6</td><td>300</td></tr>
<tr><td>15.</td><td>THE|COLORFUL|FOLK|DANCES|OF|EARLY|AMERICAN</td><td>7</td><td>307</td></tr>
<tr><td></td><td>COLONISTS|REPRESENTED|THE|RETENTION|OF|OLD</td><td>6</td><td>313</td></tr>
<tr><td></td><td>WORLD|DANCES|THAT|HAD|BEEN|IMPORTED|BY|THE</td><td>8</td><td>321</td></tr>
<tr><td></td><td>EARLY|SETTLERS|ALTHOUGH|MOST|OF|THESE|DANCES|HAVE</td><td>8</td><td>329</td></tr>
<tr><td></td><td>PASSED|INTO|OBLIVION|RECOGNIZABLE|TRACES|OF</td><td>6</td><td>335</td></tr>
<tr><td></td><td>THIS|TRADITION|PERSIST|IN|SECLUDED|REGIONS|THAT|HAVE</td><td>8</td><td>343</td></tr>
<tr><td></td><td>RETAINED|THEIR|ANCESTRAL|CHARACTER</td><td>4</td><td>347</td></tr>
<tr><td>16.</td><td>ALTHOUGH|INDOLENCE|AND|PROCRASTINATION|WERE</td><td>5</td><td>352</td></tr>
<tr><td></td><td>INHERENT|IN|HER|CONSTITUTION|SHE|PROSPERED|IN</td><td>7</td><td>359</td></tr>
<tr><td></td><td>LEARNING|THROUGH|THE|SHEER|VIGOR|OF|HER|MENTAL</td><td>8</td><td>367</td></tr>
<tr><td></td><td>PROWESS|FROM|AN|EARLY|AGE|SHE|WAS|UNCOMMONLY</td><td>8</td><td>375</td></tr>
<tr><td></td><td>INQUISITIVE|AND|HER|MEMORY|WAS|SO|TENACIOUS|THAT</td><td>8</td><td>383</td></tr>
<tr><td></td><td>HER|MENTORS|WERE|FOREVER|INCREDULOUS|AT|HER</td><td>7</td><td>390</td></tr>
<tr><td></td><td>POWERS|OF|RETENTION</td><td>3</td><td>393</td></tr>
<tr><td>17.</td><td>AS|A|POET|THE|INDEFATIGABLE|YOUNG|MAN|SEEMS|TO</td><td>9</td><td>402</td></tr>
<tr><td></td><td>OCCUPY|AN|INDETERMINATE|POSITION|BETWEEN|THE</td><td>6</td><td>408</td></tr>
<tr><td></td><td>TRANSCENDENTALISTS|AND|THE|EXTENSIVE|BODY|OF</td><td>6</td><td>414</td></tr>
<tr><td></td><td>VERSIFIERS|WHO|ADDRESS|THE|MEEK|INTELLECT|AND</td><td>7</td><td>421</td></tr>
<tr><td></td><td>SYMPATHIES|OF|THE|MULTITUDE|HIS|POEMS|TO|ACCORD</td><td>8</td><td>429</td></tr>
<tr><td></td><td>THEM|THEIR|DUE|ARE|NOT|TOTALLY|DEVOID|OF|MEANING</td><td>9</td><td>438</td></tr>
</table>

For Scoring Exercises Only

Form D

		Line Word Count	Total Word Count
1.	I RIDE	2	2
2.	COME NOW	2	4
3.	GO HERE LOOK UP	4	8
4.	FIND HIM STAY HERE	4	12
5.	IT WAS THE DAY FOR THE SCHOOL PICNIC ALL THE FOOD WAS	12	24
	ON A TABLE UNDER A TREE	6	30
6.	WHEN THE CHILDREN WERE READY THEY HELPED THEIR	8	38
	FATHER LOOK FOR THE CAR KEYS MOTHER KISSED THEM	9	47
	ALL AND SAID HAVE A NICE DAY	7	54
7.	ONE DAY SOME CHILDREN WERE PLAYING IN THE SNOW THEY	10	64
	WERE MAKING SNOW ANIMALS	4	68
8.	IT WAS PET DAY AT THE STATE FAIR UNDER THE BIG PINK	12	80
	TENT THE CHILDREN WERE WAITING FOR THE PARADE OF	9	89
	ANIMALS TO BEGIN	3	92
9.	IT IS DIFFICULT FOR ANYTHING TO LIVE IN A DESERT MANY	11	103
	DESERT ANIMALS SPEND MUCH OF THEIR TIME SEARCHING	8	111
	FOR WATER HOLES	3	114
10.	AN ELEPHANT WAS WALKING THROUGH THE JUNGLE ALONE	8	122
	FRIGHTENED THAT HE MIGHT COME UPON A SNAKE HE HAD	10	132
	NEVER SEEN A SNAKE BEFORE BUT HE HAD HEARD WHAT	10	142
	TERRIBLE CREATURES THEY WERE	4	146
11.	SHE LED GROUPS OF SLAVES FROM ONE POINT TO ANOTHER	10	156
	ON THE PERILOUS JOURNEY NORTH THEY TRAVELED ONLY	8	164
	AFTER NIGHTFALL HIDING DURING THE DAY IN BASEMENTS	8	172
	FIELDS AND FORESTS	3	175

<table>
<tr><th></th><th></th><th>Line Word Count</th><th>Total Word Count</th></tr>
<tr><td>12.</td><td>CIVILIAN|AIRPLANE|PILOTS|HAVE|MANY|IMPORTANT|JOBS</td><td>7</td><td>182</td></tr>
<tr><td></td><td>THEY|TRANSPORT|PASSENGERS|FREIGHT|AND|MAIL|FROM</td><td>7</td><td>189</td></tr>
<tr><td></td><td>ONE|CITY|TO|ANOTHER</td><td>4</td><td>193</td></tr>
<tr><td>13.</td><td>AS|I|LISTENED|TO|MY|GRANDFATHER|REMINISCING|ABOUT</td><td>8</td><td>201</td></tr>
<tr><td></td><td>HIS|PAST|I|SAW|HIM|IN|A|NEW|LIGHT|THERE|WAS|A|TONE|IN|HIS</td><td>15</td><td>216</td></tr>
<tr><td></td><td>VOICE|AS|HE|SPOKE|OF|HIS|FAMILY|AND|FRIENDS|THAT</td><td>10</td><td>226</td></tr>
<tr><td></td><td>CONVEYED|A|SENSITIVITY|AND|VULNERABILITY|THAT|I|HAD</td><td>8</td><td>234</td></tr>
<tr><td></td><td>NOT|SEEN|BEFORE</td><td>3</td><td>237</td></tr>
<tr><td>14.</td><td>THE|LIFE|OF|A|MOVIE|STAR|IS|RARELY|AS|GLAMOROUS|AS|WE</td><td>12</td><td>249</td></tr>
<tr><td></td><td>IMAGINE|MOST|STARS|SPEND|COUNTLESS|HOURS|STUDYING</td><td>7</td><td>256</td></tr>
<tr><td></td><td>THEIR|LINES|TAKING|ACTING|LESSONS|AND|PRACTICING|ALL</td><td>8</td><td>264</td></tr>
<tr><td></td><td>THE|SKILLS|NECESSARY|FOR|A|CAREER|IN|SHOW|BUSINESS</td><td>9</td><td>273</td></tr>
<tr><td></td><td>SUCH|AS|SINGING|AND|DANCING</td><td>5</td><td>278</td></tr>
<tr><td>15.</td><td>AS|THE|YOUNG|WOMAN|AWAITED|LIFTOFF|ABOARD|THE|SPACE</td><td>9</td><td>287</td></tr>
<tr><td></td><td>SHUTTLE|SHE|REFLECTED|ON|THE|STIFF|TRAINING|PROGRAM</td><td>8</td><td>295</td></tr>
<tr><td></td><td>THAT|HAD|PREPARED|HER|FOR|HER|FIRST|SPACE|FLIGHT</td><td>9</td><td>304</td></tr>
<tr><td></td><td>UNLIKE|MOST|CAREER|ASTRONAUTS|SHE|HAD|BEEN|SELECTED</td><td>8</td><td>312</td></tr>
<tr><td></td><td>FOR|THE|FLIGHT|BECAUSE|OF|HER|PHYSICS|BACKGROUND</td><td>8</td><td>320</td></tr>
<tr><td></td><td>RATHER|THAN|HER|AVIATION|EXPERIENCE</td><td>5</td><td>325</td></tr>
<tr><td>16.</td><td>THE|FUNCTION|OF|CHILDRENS|GAMES|HAS|RECENTLY|GAINED</td><td>8</td><td>333</td></tr>
<tr><td></td><td>IMPORTANCE|AS|A|SUBJECT|OF|INVESTIGATION|IN|THE|SOCIAL</td><td>9</td><td>342</td></tr>
<tr><td></td><td>SCIENCES|GAMES|PARTICULARLY|THOSE|THAT|ACCENTUATE</td><td>6</td><td>348</td></tr>
<tr><td></td><td>RHYME|RHYTHM|OR|DRAMATIC|ACTION|CATER|TO|AN|INNATE</td><td>9</td><td>357</td></tr>
<tr><td></td><td>NEED|TO|ENGAGE|IN|IMAGINATIVE|AND|EXPRESSIVE|BEHAVIOR</td><td>8</td><td>365</td></tr>
<tr><td>17.</td><td>IF|THERE|WAS|ANY|OVERTURE|OF|PEACE|THE|AMBASSADOR</td><td>9</td><td>374</td></tr>
<tr><td></td><td>WAS|EXCEEDINGLY|VIGILANT|AND|SOLICITOUS|TO|PRESS</td><td>7</td><td>381</td></tr>
<tr><td></td><td>ANYTHNG|THAT|HE|THOUGHT|MIGHT|SECURE|IT|SITTING</td><td>8</td><td>389</td></tr>
<tr><td></td><td>WITH|HIS|COHORTS|HE|WOULD|FERVENTLY|CONFESS</td><td>7</td><td>396</td></tr>
<tr><td></td><td>THAT|THE|ATROCITIES|OF|THE|WAR|AND|THE|DEVASTATION</td><td>9</td><td>405</td></tr>
<tr><td></td><td>THAT|HAD|BEFALLEN|THE|KINGDOM|ROBBED|HIM|NIGHTLY|OF</td><td>9</td><td>414</td></tr>
<tr><td></td><td>HIS|REPOSE|AND|WOULD|SHORTLY|REND|HIS|HEART|ASUNDER</td><td>9</td><td>423</td></tr>
</table>

For Scoring Exercises Only

Table A.2: Converting Raw Scores to Grade Equivelents

Grade Equivalent	Form A	Form B	Form C	Form D	Grade Equivalent
1.0	25–28	25–28	25–28	25–33	1.0
1.2	29–31	29–32	29–32	34–37	1.2
1.4	32–35	33–36	33–36	38–42	1.4
1.7	36–40	37–40	37–41	43–47	1.7
2.0	41–43	41–44	42–45	48–50	2.0
2.2	44–47	45–47	46–49	51–55	2.2
2.4	48–50	48–51	50–54	56–59	2.4
2.7	51–53	52–54	55–57	60–63	2.7
3.0	54–58	55–58	58–61	64–68	3.0
3.2	59–61	59–62	62–65	69–71	3.2
3.4	62–65	63–65	66–69	72–75	3.4
3.7	66–68	66–69	70–73	76–80	3.7
4.0	69–72	70–73	74–77	81–83	4.0
4.2	73–75	74–76	78–80	84–87	4.2
4.4	76–79	77–79	81–83	88–90	4.4
4.7	80–82	80–82	84–87	91–93	4.7
5.0	83–84	83–84	88–90	94–96	5.0
5.2	85–86	85–87	91–93	97–100	5.2
5.4	87–88	88–90	94–97	101–103	5.4
5.7	89–93	91–93	98–100	104–107	5.7
6.0	94–96	94–96	101–103	108–110	6.0
6.2	97–99	97–99	104–106	111–113	6.2
6.4	100–101	100–102	107–109	114–116	6.4
6.7	102–104	103–104	110–112	117–119	6.7
7.0	105–107	105–107	113–115	120–121	7.0
7.2	108–110	108–109	116–117	122–124	7.2
7.4	111–112	110–111	118–120	125–126	7.4
7.7	113–114	112–114	121–122	127–129	7.7

(Continued on next page)

Grade Equivalent	Form				Grade Equivalent
	A	B	C	D	
8.0	115–117	115–117	123–125	130–131	8.0
8.2	118–119	118–119	126–127	132–134	8.2
8.4	120–122	120–121	128–129	135–136	8.4
8.7	123–124	122–123	130–131	137–138	8.7
9.0	125–126	124–125	132–134	139–140	9.0
9.2	127–128	126–127	135–136	141–143	9.2
9.4	129–130	128–129	137	144–145	9.4
9.7	131–132	130–131	138–140	146	9.7
10.0	133–134	132–133	141	147–148	10.0
10.2	135–136	134–135	142–143	149–150	10.2
10.4	137–138	136	144–145	151	10.4
10.7	139	137–138	146	152–153	10.7
11.0	140–141	139–140	147–148	154	11.0
11.2	142–143	141–142	149–150	155–156	11.2
11.4	144–145	143	151	157	11.4
11.7	146	144–145	152	158–159	11.7
12.0	147	146	153–154	160	12.0
12.2	148–149	147	155	161	12.2
12.4	150	148	156	162	12.4
12.7	151–152	149–150	157–158	163	12.7
13.0	·152	·150	·158	·163	13.0

Appendix B

- Class Rosters

Content Mastery Task Class Roster for Book A

Unit: 1 2 3 4 5 6 (circle one)

Student Name	Content Mastery Task									
	Step 1 Learning the Code		Step 2 Spelling Posttest 1		Step 2 Spelling Posttest 2		Step 3 Vocabulary and Morphology		Step 4 Grammar and Usage	
	# Correct	% Correct[a]	# Correct	% Correct[a]	# Correct	% Correct[a]	# Correct	% Correct[a]	# Correct	% Correct[a]
	/10		/10		/5		/5		/10	
	/10		/10		/5		/5		/10	
	/10		/10		/5		/5		/10	
	/10		/10		/5		/5		/10	
	/10		/10		/5		/5		/10	
	/10		/10		/5		/5		/10	
	/10		/10		/5		/5		/10	
	/10		/10		/5		/5		/10	
	/10		/10		/5		/5		/10	
	/10		/10		/5		/5		/10	
	/10		/10		/5		/5		/10	
	/10		/10		/5		/5		/10	
	/10		/10		/5		/5		/10	
	/10		/10		/5		/5		/10	
	/10		/10		/5		/5		/10	
	/10		/10		/5		/5		/10	
	/10		/10		/5		/5		/10	
	/10		/10		/5		/5		/10	
	/10		/10		/5		/5		/10	
	/10		/10		/5		/5		/10	
	/10		/10		/5		/5		/10	
	/10		/10		/5		/5		/10	
	/10		/10		/5		/5		/10	
	/10		/10		/5		/5		/10	

[a]Students should achieve 80 percent. When performance falls below 80 percent, review, reteach, or emphasize the skills covered by the task in the next unit.

[b]Students should achieve an average rating of at least 4.0 to demonstrate proficient performance on the task.

End-of-Book Content Mastery Task Class Roster for Book A

Student Name	Date	**Step 1:** Word Study		**Step 3:** Vocabulary		**Step 3:** Word Relationships		**Step 3:** Morphology		**Step 4:** Grammar		**Step 4:** Sentence Structure		**Steps 1, 3, and 4:** Total Score	
		# Acc	% Acc[a]	# Acc	% Acc[a]	# Acc	% Acc[a]	# Acc	% Acc[a]	# Acc	% Acc[a]	# Acc	% Acc[a]	Total Acc	Overall % Acc[b]
		/5		/10		/5		/10		/10		/10		/50	
		/5		/10		/5		/10		/10		/10		/50	
		/5		/10		/5		/10		/10		/10		/50	
		/5		/10		/5		/10		/10		/10		/50	
		/5		/10		/5		/10		/10		/10		/50	
		/5		/10		/5		/10		/10		/10		/50	
		/5		/10		/5		/10		/10		/10		/50	
		/5		/10		/5		/10		/10		/10		/50	
		/5		/10		/5		/10		/10		/10		/50	
		/5		/10		/5		/10		/10		/10		/50	
		/5		/10		/5		/10		/10		/10		/50	
		/5		/10		/5		/10		/10		/10		/50	
		/5		/10		/5		/10		/10		/10		/50	
		/5		/10		/5		/10		/10		/10		/50	
		/5		/10		/5		/10		/10		/10		/50	
		/5		/10		/5		/10		/10		/10		/50	
		/5		/10		/5		/10		/10		/10		/50	
		/5		/10		/5		/10		/10		/10		/50	
		/5		/10		/5		/10		/10		/10		/50	
		/5		/10		/5		/10		/10		/10		/50	
		/5		/10		/5		/10		/10		/10		/50	
		/5		/10		/5		/10		/10		/10		/50	
		/5		/10		/5		/10		/10		/10		/50	
		/5		/10		/5		/10		/10		/10		/50	

[a]Students should achieve at least 80 percent on individual sections of the Summative Test. When performance falls below 80 percent, review, reteach, and/or emphasize the skills covered by the section in Book A.

[b]Students should achieve at least 85 percent on overall performance to pass and demonstrate adequate progress toward instructional goals.

Appendix B

Baseline and Progress Indicator Class Roster for Book A

	Test Date (MM/DD/YY)		TOSCRF Grade Equivalent		LRS Lexile®		TWS-4 Grade Equivalent	
Student Name	Baseline Form A	Progress Indicator Form B	Baseline Form A	Progress Indicator Form B	Baseline Form A	Progress Indicator Form B	Baseline Form A	Progress Indicator Form B

Baseline, Benchmark and Progress Indicator Class Roster for Book A: Writing

	Test Date (MM/DD/YY)				Ideas and Content			
Student Name	Baseline	Benchmark Unit 2	Benchmark Unit 4	Progress Indicator	Baseline	Benchmark Unit 2	Benchmark Unit 4	Progress Indicator

(Continued on next page)

Baseline, Benchmark and Progress Indicator Class Roster for Book A: Writing *(cont.)*

	Organization				Voice and Audience Awareness			
Student Name	Baseline	Benchmark Unit 2	Benchmark Unit 4	Progress Indicator	Baseline	Benchmark Unit 2	Benchmark Unit 4	Progress Indicator

(Continued on next page)

Baseline, Benchmark and Progress Indicator Class Roster for Book A: Writing *(cont.)*

	Word Choice				Sentence Fluency			
Student Name	Baseline	Benchmark Unit 2	Benchmark Unit 4	Progress Indicator	Baseline	Benchmark Unit 2	Benchmark Unit 4	Progress Indicator

(Continued on next page)

Baseline, Benchmark and Progress Indicator Class Roster for Book A: Writing *(cont.)*

	Conventions (Average rating for capitalization and punctuation, grammar and usage, and spelling)			
Student Name	Baseline	Benchmark Unit 2	Benchmark Unit 4	Progress Indicator

Appendix C

- LRS Student Answer Forms and Keys

Appendix C

Name_________________________________ Date_______________

LRS Student Answer Form—Baseline for Book A

S-1 Ⓐ Ⓑ ● Ⓓ	S-2 Ⓐ Ⓑ Ⓒ Ⓓ	
1. Ⓐ Ⓑ Ⓒ Ⓓ	18. Ⓐ Ⓑ Ⓒ Ⓓ	35. Ⓐ Ⓑ Ⓒ Ⓓ
2. Ⓐ Ⓑ Ⓒ Ⓓ	19. Ⓐ Ⓑ Ⓒ Ⓓ	36. Ⓐ Ⓑ Ⓒ Ⓓ
3. Ⓐ Ⓑ Ⓒ Ⓓ	20. Ⓐ Ⓑ Ⓒ Ⓓ	37. Ⓐ Ⓑ Ⓒ Ⓓ
4. Ⓐ Ⓑ Ⓒ Ⓓ	21. Ⓐ Ⓑ Ⓒ Ⓓ	38. Ⓐ Ⓑ Ⓒ Ⓓ
5. Ⓐ Ⓑ Ⓒ Ⓓ	22. Ⓐ Ⓑ Ⓒ Ⓓ	39. Ⓐ Ⓑ Ⓒ Ⓓ
6. Ⓐ Ⓑ Ⓒ Ⓓ	23. Ⓐ Ⓑ Ⓒ Ⓓ	40. Ⓐ Ⓑ Ⓒ Ⓓ
7. Ⓐ Ⓑ Ⓒ Ⓓ	24. Ⓐ Ⓑ Ⓒ Ⓓ	41. Ⓐ Ⓑ Ⓒ Ⓓ
8. Ⓐ Ⓑ Ⓒ Ⓓ	25. Ⓐ Ⓑ Ⓒ Ⓓ	42. Ⓐ Ⓑ Ⓒ Ⓓ
9. Ⓐ Ⓑ Ⓒ Ⓓ	26. Ⓐ Ⓑ Ⓒ Ⓓ	43. Ⓐ Ⓑ Ⓒ Ⓓ
10. Ⓐ Ⓑ Ⓒ Ⓓ	27. Ⓐ Ⓑ Ⓒ Ⓓ	44. Ⓐ Ⓑ Ⓒ Ⓓ
11. Ⓐ Ⓑ Ⓒ Ⓓ	28. Ⓐ Ⓑ Ⓒ Ⓓ	45. Ⓐ Ⓑ Ⓒ Ⓓ
12. Ⓐ Ⓑ Ⓒ Ⓓ	29. Ⓐ Ⓑ Ⓒ Ⓓ	46. Ⓐ Ⓑ Ⓒ Ⓓ
13. Ⓐ Ⓑ Ⓒ Ⓓ	30. Ⓐ Ⓑ Ⓒ Ⓓ	47. Ⓐ Ⓑ Ⓒ Ⓓ
14. Ⓐ Ⓑ Ⓒ Ⓓ	31. Ⓐ Ⓑ Ⓒ Ⓓ	48. Ⓐ Ⓑ Ⓒ Ⓓ
15. Ⓐ Ⓑ Ⓒ Ⓓ	32. Ⓐ Ⓑ Ⓒ Ⓓ	49. Ⓐ Ⓑ Ⓒ Ⓓ
16. Ⓐ Ⓑ Ⓒ Ⓓ	33. Ⓐ Ⓑ Ⓒ Ⓓ	
17. Ⓐ Ⓑ Ⓒ Ⓓ	34. Ⓐ Ⓑ Ⓒ Ⓓ	

Name ______________________________ Date ______________

LRS Student Answer Form—Progress Indicator for Book A

S-1 Ⓐ Ⓑ ● Ⓓ	S-2 Ⓐ Ⓑ Ⓒ Ⓓ	
1. Ⓐ Ⓑ Ⓒ Ⓓ	18. Ⓐ Ⓑ Ⓒ Ⓓ	35. Ⓐ Ⓑ Ⓒ Ⓓ
2. Ⓐ Ⓑ Ⓒ Ⓓ	19. Ⓐ Ⓑ Ⓒ Ⓓ	36. Ⓐ Ⓑ Ⓒ Ⓓ
3. Ⓐ Ⓑ Ⓒ Ⓓ	20. Ⓐ Ⓑ Ⓒ Ⓓ	37. Ⓐ Ⓑ Ⓒ Ⓓ
4. Ⓐ Ⓑ Ⓒ Ⓓ	21. Ⓐ Ⓑ Ⓒ Ⓓ	38. Ⓐ Ⓑ Ⓒ Ⓓ
5. Ⓐ Ⓑ Ⓒ Ⓓ	22. Ⓐ Ⓑ Ⓒ Ⓓ	39. Ⓐ Ⓑ Ⓒ Ⓓ
6. Ⓐ Ⓑ Ⓒ Ⓓ	23. Ⓐ Ⓑ Ⓒ Ⓓ	40. Ⓐ Ⓑ Ⓒ Ⓓ
7. Ⓐ Ⓑ Ⓒ Ⓓ	24. Ⓐ Ⓑ Ⓒ Ⓓ	41. Ⓐ Ⓑ Ⓒ Ⓓ
8. Ⓐ Ⓑ Ⓒ Ⓓ	25. Ⓐ Ⓑ Ⓒ Ⓓ	42. Ⓐ Ⓑ Ⓒ Ⓓ
9. Ⓐ Ⓑ Ⓒ Ⓓ	26. Ⓐ Ⓑ Ⓒ Ⓓ	43. Ⓐ Ⓑ Ⓒ Ⓓ
10. Ⓐ Ⓑ Ⓒ Ⓓ	27. Ⓐ Ⓑ Ⓒ Ⓓ	44. Ⓐ Ⓑ Ⓒ Ⓓ
11. Ⓐ Ⓑ Ⓒ Ⓓ	28. Ⓐ Ⓑ Ⓒ Ⓓ	45. Ⓐ Ⓑ Ⓒ Ⓓ
12. Ⓐ Ⓑ Ⓒ Ⓓ	29. Ⓐ Ⓑ Ⓒ Ⓓ	46. Ⓐ Ⓑ Ⓒ Ⓓ
13. Ⓐ Ⓑ Ⓒ Ⓓ	30. Ⓐ Ⓑ Ⓒ Ⓓ	47. Ⓐ Ⓑ Ⓒ Ⓓ
14. Ⓐ Ⓑ Ⓒ Ⓓ	31. Ⓐ Ⓑ Ⓒ Ⓓ	48. Ⓐ Ⓑ Ⓒ Ⓓ
15. Ⓐ Ⓑ Ⓒ Ⓓ	32. Ⓐ Ⓑ Ⓒ Ⓓ	49. Ⓐ Ⓑ Ⓒ Ⓓ
16. Ⓐ Ⓑ Ⓒ Ⓓ	33. Ⓐ Ⓑ Ⓒ Ⓓ	
17. Ⓐ Ⓑ Ⓒ Ⓓ	34. Ⓐ Ⓑ Ⓒ Ⓓ	

Appendix C

Photocopy this page on a transparency to make a LRS scoring overlay to use with the LRS student answer form.

LRS Student Answer Form Key—Baseline for Book A

S-1 Ⓐ Ⓑ ● Ⓓ	**S-2** ● Ⓑ Ⓒ Ⓓ	
1. Ⓐ Ⓑ Ⓒ ●	18. Ⓐ Ⓑ ● Ⓓ	35. Ⓐ Ⓑ Ⓒ ●
2. Ⓐ ● Ⓒ Ⓓ	19. ● Ⓑ Ⓒ Ⓓ	36. Ⓐ Ⓑ Ⓒ ●
3. Ⓐ ● Ⓒ Ⓓ	20. Ⓐ Ⓑ ● Ⓓ	37. Ⓐ Ⓑ ● Ⓓ
4. Ⓐ Ⓑ ● Ⓓ	21. Ⓐ Ⓑ Ⓒ ●	38. Ⓐ Ⓑ Ⓒ ●
5. ● Ⓑ Ⓒ Ⓓ	22. Ⓐ Ⓑ Ⓒ ●	39. ● Ⓑ Ⓒ Ⓓ
6. ● Ⓑ Ⓒ Ⓓ	23. Ⓐ Ⓑ ● Ⓓ	40. Ⓐ ● Ⓒ Ⓓ
7. Ⓐ ● Ⓒ Ⓓ	24. Ⓐ Ⓑ ● Ⓓ	41. Ⓐ ● Ⓒ Ⓓ
8. ● Ⓑ Ⓒ Ⓓ	25. Ⓐ ● Ⓒ Ⓓ	42. Ⓐ Ⓑ ● Ⓓ
9. ● Ⓑ Ⓒ Ⓓ	26. ● Ⓑ Ⓒ Ⓓ	43. Ⓐ Ⓑ ● Ⓓ
10. Ⓐ Ⓑ Ⓒ ●	27. ● Ⓑ Ⓒ Ⓓ	44. Ⓐ Ⓑ Ⓒ ●
11. Ⓐ Ⓑ Ⓒ ●	28. Ⓐ Ⓑ ● Ⓓ	45. Ⓐ Ⓑ ● Ⓓ
12. Ⓐ Ⓑ ● Ⓓ	29. Ⓐ ● Ⓒ Ⓓ	46. ● Ⓑ Ⓒ Ⓓ
13. Ⓐ ● Ⓒ Ⓓ	30. ● Ⓑ Ⓒ Ⓓ	47. Ⓐ Ⓑ ● Ⓓ
14. Ⓐ ● Ⓒ Ⓓ	31. Ⓐ ● Ⓒ Ⓓ	48. Ⓐ Ⓑ Ⓒ ●
15. Ⓐ Ⓑ Ⓒ ●	32. Ⓐ Ⓑ ● Ⓓ	49. Ⓐ ● Ⓒ Ⓓ
16. Ⓐ ● Ⓒ Ⓓ	33. Ⓐ ● Ⓒ Ⓓ	
17. ● Ⓑ Ⓒ Ⓓ	34. Ⓐ Ⓑ Ⓒ ●	

Photocopy this page on a transparency to make a LRS scoring overlay to use with the LRS student answer form.

LRS Student Answer Form Key—Progress Indicator for Book A

S-1	S-2	
Ⓐ Ⓑ ● Ⓓ	● Ⓑ Ⓒ Ⓓ	
1. Ⓐ Ⓑ ● Ⓓ	18. Ⓐ ● Ⓒ Ⓓ	35. Ⓐ Ⓑ Ⓒ ●
2. Ⓐ Ⓑ Ⓒ ●	19. Ⓐ Ⓑ ● Ⓓ	36. Ⓐ Ⓑ ● Ⓓ
3. ● Ⓑ Ⓒ Ⓓ	20. Ⓐ Ⓑ Ⓒ ●	37. Ⓐ Ⓑ ● Ⓓ
4. Ⓐ Ⓑ ● Ⓓ	21. ● Ⓑ Ⓒ Ⓓ	38. Ⓐ ● Ⓒ Ⓓ
5. Ⓐ ● Ⓒ Ⓓ	22. ● Ⓑ Ⓒ Ⓓ	39. ● Ⓑ Ⓒ Ⓓ
6. Ⓐ ● Ⓒ Ⓓ	23. Ⓐ Ⓑ ● Ⓓ	40. ● Ⓑ Ⓒ Ⓓ
7. ● Ⓑ Ⓒ Ⓓ	24. Ⓐ Ⓑ ● Ⓓ	41. Ⓐ Ⓑ Ⓒ ●
8. ● Ⓑ Ⓒ Ⓓ	25. Ⓐ ● Ⓒ Ⓓ	42. Ⓐ Ⓑ Ⓒ ●
9. Ⓐ ● Ⓒ Ⓓ	26. ● Ⓑ Ⓒ Ⓓ	43. Ⓐ ● Ⓒ Ⓓ
10. ● Ⓑ Ⓒ Ⓓ	27. ● Ⓑ Ⓒ Ⓓ	44. Ⓐ Ⓑ Ⓒ ●
11. Ⓐ Ⓑ Ⓒ ●	28. Ⓐ ● Ⓒ Ⓓ	45. Ⓐ Ⓑ ● Ⓓ
12. Ⓐ Ⓑ ● Ⓓ	29. Ⓐ Ⓑ Ⓒ ●	46. Ⓐ Ⓑ Ⓒ ●
13. Ⓐ Ⓑ Ⓒ ●	30. ● Ⓑ Ⓒ Ⓓ	47. ● Ⓑ Ⓒ Ⓓ
14. Ⓐ ● Ⓒ Ⓓ	31. ● Ⓑ Ⓒ Ⓓ	48. Ⓐ ● Ⓒ Ⓓ
15. Ⓐ ● Ⓒ Ⓓ	32. Ⓐ Ⓑ ● Ⓓ	49. Ⓐ Ⓑ ● Ⓓ
16. Ⓐ Ⓑ Ⓒ ●	33. Ⓐ ● Ⓒ Ⓓ	
17. Ⓐ Ⓑ Ⓒ ●	34. Ⓐ ● Ⓒ Ⓓ	

Appendix D

- References

Appendix D

References

Anastasi, A., & Urbina, S. (1997). *Psychological testing* (7th ed.). Upper Saddle River, NJ: Prentice Hall.

Bear, D. R., Invernizzi, M., Templeton, S. R., & Johnston, F. (2000). *Words their way: Word study for phonics, vocabulary, and spelling instruction* (2nd ed.). Upper Saddle River, NJ: Pearson Education.

Bracken, B. A. (1987). Limitations of preschool instruments for minimal levels of technical adequacy. *Journal of Psychoeducational Assessment*, 4, 313–326.

Hammill, D. D., Wiederholt, J. L., & Allen, E. A. (2006) *Test of Silent Contextual Reading Fluency*. Austin, TX: PRO-ED.

Larsen, S.C., Hammill, D. D., & Moats, L. C. (1999). *Test of Written Spelling–Fourth Edition*. Austin, TX: PRO-ED.

Linn, R. L., & Miller, M. D. (2005). *Measurement and assessment in teaching* (9th ed.). Upper Saddle River, NJ: Pearson Education.

Lyman, H. B. (1998). *Test scores and what they mean* (6th ed.). Englewood Cliffs, NJ: Prentice Hall.

Mather, N., Hammill, D. D., Allen, E. A., & Roberts, R. (2004). *Test of Silent Word Reading Fluency*. Austin, TX: PRO-ED.

McLoughlin, J. A., & Lewis, R. B. (2001). *Assessing students with special needs* (5th ed.). Upper Saddle River, NJ: Merrill/Prentice Hall.

Rathvon, N. (2004). *Early reading assessment*. New York: Guilford Press.

Salvia, J., & Ysseldyke, J. E. (2001). *Assessment* (8th ed.). Boston: Houghton-Mifflin.

Torgesen, J. K., Wagner, R., & Rashotte, C. A. (1999). *Test of Word Reading Efficiency*. Austin, TX: PRO-ED.

U.S. Bureau of the Census. (1997). *Statistical abstract of the United States*. Washington, DC: Author.

Wechsler, D. (2003). *Wechsler Intelligence Scale for Children–Fourth Edition*. San Antonio: Psychological Corp.

Wiederholt, J. L., & Blalock, G. (2000). *Gray Silent Reading Tests*. Austin, TX: PRO-ED.

Wiederholt, J. L., & Bryant, B. R. (2001). *Gray Oral Reading Tests–Fourth Edition*. Austin, TX: PRO-ED.

Woodcock, R. W., McGrew, K. S., & Mather, N. (2001). *Woodcock–Johnson III*. Itasca, IL: Riverside.